THEATRE AND STAGE SERIES

General Editor: HAROLD DOWNS

THE ART OF
DRAMATIC CRITICISM

THE ART OF
DRAMATIC CRITICISM

BY

S. R. LITTLEWOOD

WITH A FOREWORD BY

SIR BARRY JACKSON

LONDON
SIR ISAAC PITMAN & SONS, LTD.

First published 1952

SIR ISAAC PITMAN & SONS, Ltd.
PITMAN HOUSE, PARKER STREET, KINGSWAY, LONDON, W.C.2
THE PITMAN PRESS, BATH
PITMAN HOUSE, LITTLE COLLINS STREET, MELBOURNE
27 BECKETTS BUILDINGS, PRESIDENT STREET, JOHANNESBURG

ASSOCIATED COMPANIES
PITMAN PUBLISHING CORPORATION
2 WEST 45TH STREET, NEW YORK

SIR ISAAC PITMAN & SONS (CANADA), Ltd.
(INCORPORATING THE COMMERCIAL TEXT BOOK COMPANY)
PITMAN HOUSE, 381–383 CHURCH STREET, TORONTO

MADE IN GREAT BRITAIN AT THE PITMAN PRESS, BATH
E2—(G.412)

FOREWORD

TENDENCIES in modern journalism and abnormal circumstances in newspaper production have tended to limit
the quantity of dramatic criticism that is regularly published
to appeal to theatregoers. This must be deplored, but fortunately the quality in periodicals of culture continues to be
characteristic of serious-minded students and specialists whose
love of the contemporary theatre is as warm and as deep as
their knowledge of it. One result is that theatregoing is aug-
mented by the reading of authoritative books such as Mr.
Littlewood's *Dramatic Criticism*, first published in 1939. It is
not surprising, therefore, that the edition was soon exhausted,
when uncontrollable and irremovable circumstances made
publishing increasingly difficult. It is altogether laudable
that, at the first convenient opportunity, the author revised,
enlarged, and brought his exposition up to date, and that the
publishers decided to make it available with a new and, I
think, a better title—THE ART OF DRAMATIC CRITICISM.

We who work in the theatre as producers and actors alternate
between two widely divergent views on the subject of dramatic
critics. I can certainly confess to having shared both at
different times. One—when they praise our work—is that
they are men of taste, erudition, and discernment, splendidly
upholding the traditions of that great calling which, as Mr.
Littlewood shows us, has in some sense existed since classic
times; the other—when they condemn some production on
which the manager and the actors have centred all their hopes
and to which they have given untold thought, hard work, and
expenditure—is that they are ignorant, shallow-pated bigots,
incapable of fair judgment or indeed of any judgment at all,
frivolous by nature, and further corrupted by nameless agencies
of self-interest, jealousy, and intrigue.

The truth must obviously lie between these two extremes,
and in Mr. Littlewood we have the ideal guide to show us
where it lies. No one could be better equipped for the task he
has set himself in this very interesting and valuable study of

critical problems and the critic's duties, merits, and necessary limitations.

No West-End first night for a good many years was complete without his genial, cheerful presence. Nor did he, as some of his colleagues are perhaps inclined to do, fall a victim to the delusion that the theatre begins and ends within the four-mile cab radius. We are glad to remember that he made many a voyage of discovery to our theatre in Birmingham, and to the other provincial centres where London's drama is often born; and events like the Stratford on Avon and other Festivals were for a long period inconceivable without him.

It is not alone his wide knowledge of the drama and stage-history, or a critical sense which he can as well apply to films or books, that is the secret of his success and of his popularity, even with those who from time to time bear his strictures. It is a very real passion for what is best in the theatre that shines through his writings as it informs his conversation. One too often suspects dramatic critics of despising or even positively disliking the theatre; to the jaundiced eye of the criticized a triumphant venom seems to intensify the sting of their blame, while an air of lofty and kindly patronage dilutes the perfume of their praise.

Loving the theatre, Mr. Littlewood is intolerant of dull or slipshod work, and rightly so. On the other hand, when he approves, his pen glows with appreciation, and one can tell that he is infinitely happier throwing bouquets than hurling bricks. Even in the worst play he is always eager to find some redeeming feature if it is there to be found, and many young beginners, now famous, have been helped and encouraged when S. R. L.'s eye has spotted them in a small part and cited them as a bright flash in a tedious evening.

But Mr. Littlewood would be the first to condemn an over-long prologue to a fascinating play, so it is time to "black out" on myself and ring up the curtain on a book which everyone working in the theatre or in critical journalism ought to read and will enjoy reading.

BARRY JACKSON

PREFACE

THIS book has been prepared with a view to helping young critics and would-be critics, and deals with the practice and prospects of present-day criticism, especially in its relations both with the stage as it is to-day and with the journalism of our time.

Although to some extent it is modelled on my earlier book, *Dramatic Criticism*, which was published in 1939 as a volume of the Theatre and Stage Series, but is now out of print, it has been necessary to reconsider many circumstances unknown to earlier critics, such as the coming of the Press agent, the rivalry of radio, the use of the telephone, and the growth in numbers and importance of the repertory theatres. It thus proved necessary to treat the whole subject of criticism afresh, and the result has been that this book is so essentially different from its forerunner that it would have been misleading to call it simply a new edition of *Dramatic Criticism*. Hence its appearance as a new book under a title that will serve to differentiate it from the original work.

S. R. LITTLEWOOD

CONTENTS

ix

CHAPTER I

FROM THE 'NINETIES

THE *art* of dramatic criticism—here is a claim and, in some respects, a challenge, which may need confirmation. To most of us art implies creative expression by an artist of his own thoughts and emotions in anything he is doing. It extends to the simplest activities as to the most complex—to weeding a garden or to painting a masterpiece. A garden may be wild or trim, a masterpiece this or that colour or a blend of colours. Art is called in with the choice and its fulfilment. So with criticism. It is an activity which calls from the critic an expression of his own response to painting or music, book or dance or play or imaginative work of any kind. It is a self-portrait of his own, prompted by the achievements of others, but none the less art. Moreover, criticism of the living stage has a greater value. When the actor has passed away and the play gone out of fashion, the criticism often lives as something more permanently active than either.

Let us, then, hail critics like Lamb and Hazlitt, Archer, Walkley, Shaw, Agate, and some still living and working, as artists in the truest and most enduring sense. Nothing is falser than the common notion that a critic is merely a supposed expert whose duty is to point out what he considers to be the mistakes of actor, author, or management. This generally obvious information can frequently be conveyed, if necessary, by private correspondence. It is to the public and to posterity that criticism as an art is addressed. The art of dramatic criticism includes judgment, as the word itself demands; but it must spring from a deep and personal love of, and interest in, the theatre. Its value is the conveyance of these to its readers, inspiring them to an equally devoted recognition and remembrance.

At the same time, it is an art, not a gold-mine. As a young provincial journalist of the 'nineties, I went up to London every Saturday to "do" a couple of theatres from the gallery.

On one of these journeys I was reading *Fabian Essays* and was so struck with Bernard Shaw's writing—not this time about the theatre—that I determined that very day to go and visit him at his mother's home in Fitzroy Square, where he was then living. I had no introduction, had given him no notice of my coming, and had no right of any kind to his acquaintance. I found him in his upstairs room, cooking a meal of lentils. He had only just started as dramatic critic of *The Saturday Review* on £8 a week. Shaw gave me a delightful welcome and asked me what I was going to do as a journalist. "I want to be a dramatic critic," I said. "Don't you!" he answered "It doesn't pay." How true!

Meeting Walkley and Archer

On my first evening as an appointed London critic—this was for the now-vanished *The Morning Leader*, and it was at the first night of a very poor comedy, *Nurse*, at the old Globe in 1897—Archer introduced himself to me, and Walkley took me to the bar and bought me a drink. It was, I learned afterwards, the first time he was ever known to indulge in refreshment at the theatre. It was certainly, so far as my observation went, the last. I cannot help regarding this little courtesy to a young man of 22 on the part of these two distinguished masters of their art as something worthy to be recorded, especially as they were neither of them men of the hail-fellow-well-met type. I was to have much to do with these two men and also with J. T. Grein—that indomitable Dutch enthusiast and able and keen businessman, who was Shaw's early presenter. They joined in the founding of the Critics' Circle, about which I shall have something to say later on. Undoubtedly, between them, they were the founders of the art of dramatic criticism as it is now in this country. Shaw and his successor, the "incomparable Max," as Shaw called him, in due course gave to my chosen calling the illumination of their fame—but only as an incident. To Archer and Walkley it was something which they loved and in relation to which they expressed their most intimate sincerities. They saw the fantasies and passionate creations of the stage as a life that existed in thought not only as truly as the commonplace routine, but often a good deal more so.

There were plenty of other critics of those mid-'nineties who live pleasantly in my memory. Clement Scott must receive the credit for having brought thousands of playgoers into the theatre by his sheer gusto, eloquence, and attention to acting, scene, and production; but the lack of depth that prompted his abuse of Ibsen made the nice house in Woburn Square a sufficient reward. I remember sitting between him and dear, long-bearded old Joseph Knight, scholar and good liver, on the first night of a production at the old Princess's in Oxford Street. I expected a feast of enlightenment, but their talk was all about a game of cards they had played the night before. In those days, it is worth recalling, dramatic critics were a good deal more sociable than they are now. However low our salaries, we had to turn up almost every night in evening dress, and there were no Press agents to do the news-getting. So the recluse did not have much of a chance.

At Leisure

With all its faults and divergences the dramatic criticism of the 'nineties, even in the daily papers, was a careful, leisurely comment, mostly unsigned, putting to shame the self-advertising paragraphs of later years. The fault to-day is not always that of the critics themselves. They have to push their own publicity and to concentrate all they have to say in twenty lines or so, sent or telephoned to their office either before the last curtain is down or immediately after. In my early days *The Morning Leader* did not go to press until two in the morning, and I could write till well after midnight. I find it pleasant to recall, even now, my satisfaction in getting a column-notice of *Trelawney of the Wells* done just as twelve o'clock struck, although the chief sub-editor hailed me with—"Well, Little-wood, we've got a lot of news to-night. We don't want any of your —— stuff." With an early show there was time for a snack of supper between curtain-fall and the starting of one's notice.

I remember so well, after the first performance of *A Night Out* at the Vaudeville, adapted from *L' Hôtel du Libre Échange*, which I had seen in Paris, noticing Clement Scott descend into Romanos, presumably with a view to some attractive beverage. Usually he rode to the office either in a hansom or, on great occasions, in a brougham lent by Lord Burnham. Considering that he was frequently given a box by the managements, while we other critics were scattered about the stalls, and the gallery-boys used to watch his face to see whether they should "boo" or otherwise, his adventures after the show were of some importance. As a matter of fact, he used to say that he always took care to think out his first sentence before arriving in Fleet Street. If he had got that in his mind all was well for the "column and a bit." On this occasion what his restorative at Romanos was I do not know; but his next morning's notice began: "Oh, what a night! Oh, what a night! Oh, what a night!"

Employment Elsewhere

After seven years—1897 to 1904—as critic of *The Morning Leader*, I was "sacked" for referring to an actress as a "thin-lipped infliction." No name had been mentioned, but the paper was threatened with a libel action, especially as the lady concerned was a particular friend of the management, the suggestion being that her identity was clearly indicated—the only escape being my demanded dismissal. According to the advice of Rufus Isaacs, the future Lord Reading, then a rising young barrister, this was the better alternative for the proprietors. As a matter of fact, what looked like a disaster for me proved an altogether happy event. My case was taken up by the old *Referee*, and I became straight away a member of Richard Butler's strictly guarded Round Table, which included George R. Sims as "Dagonet," Chance Newton as "Carados," with my assistance in the opening column of criticism, and myself as "Agravaine." Very soon, too, I joined *The Daily Chronicle*, upon which I was to work for ten years, right up to the declaration of war in 1914, when Sir Robert Donald thought it a good idea to save my salary, not imagining that there was likely to be much drama in evidence. *The Morning Post*—in succession to G. E. Morrison—was to follow.

All these papers, it may be noted, have either ceased altogether or been amalgamated. There are times even now, when I reflect upon the doubtful value of work packed away in those forgotten files. Criticism thus shares the fate of the actor; but only to a point. Wherever buried, it still exists. Frequently, I and others look up my old notices. Criticism can also be published in book form, which brings it to the shelf; though the immortality which comes by some special chance—possibly by accidental reference—seems to me much the best and most natural. I do feel that while memory lasts, we had much better use it. Comparison becomes more possible.

CHAPTER II

BEGINNINGS OF CRITICISM

ONE has to admit the existence of drama and criticism long before writing. The barbarian dancers and the chief or high priest who gave his all-important opinion were for ages without any means of ensuring the survival of their ideas, save by hearsay and consequent tradition. These were, as we know, vastly effective. The amount of great drama which goes back to prehistoric origins is considerable. The story of *The Sleeping Princess*, for instance, recalls the primeval legendry of night and day. Does not the very word "comedy" take us back to the inarticulate revels of ancient villagers in the vine-harvest, and "tragedy" to the killing of a goat as an enemy of the vine or, possibly, the giving of it as a prize? The old masks, with their satyr-grins or ghastly frowns, have no relation to literature. Yet out of these grew the still supreme comedy of Aristophanes and the tragic masterpieces which hold a modern audience just as surely as they did the throng in the Greek theatre—that place of creative miracles.

Who was the first critic? Going right back to the primitive it is difficult to get away from a feeling that the first people to cherish communal expression of emotions, gay or grave, were the priests. The relation of the arts to life—of music, painting, and sculpture no less than of drama, which often links them— has in it an element of mystery to which religion serves as an interpreter. We laugh and cry, as also did primitive man, without thinking why we should indulge in needless and useless tears and laughter. An impulse for them comes to us as children, marking us out from mere animals. The interpretation of emotion arrives later as religion. In the culture of this, some priesthood has always claimed an authority handed down from generation to generation. Practically all prehistoric gatherings out of which the drama sprang had a religious basis, with priestcraft in the background. When the theatre broke away from church, temple, or tribal plot, priestly inspiration naturally declined. In a curious way the encouragement or condemnation meted out by critics has, to a certain extent, taken its place. Someone must be there to explain to the multitude why it should all happen and to express on their behalf a response of some sort.

The Passion Play of Osiris

Though hardly a criticism, the first personal account of a dramatic performance which I have been able to discover is that of the Passion Play of Osiris, performed at and near Abydos in 3000 B.C. or earlier. The account was given by the Egyptian producer himself, I-kher-nefert, who not only organized the pageant but took several of the chief parts. The play itself—symbolic, among other things, of the solar setting and rising—represented, it will be recalled, a search for the body of Osiris by his sister-wife, Isis, and son, Horus, who avenges his father's death at the hands of Set, the god of darkness.

> I performed the Great Coming Forth. . . . I provided the Lord of Abydos with a cabin-shrine and splendid apparel. I caused him (Osiris) to set out in the boat which bore his Beauty. I made the hearts of the dwellers in the East to expand with joy and caused gladness to be in the dwellers in Amentat (West), when they saw the Beauty, as it landed at Abydos, bringing Osiris, the Lord of Abydos, to his Palace.

The Passion Play of Osiris lasted for three days, the procession moving from place to place in supposed search for the body, cut into fourteen pieces. At each place was a mimic fight. Vast crowds, we are told, uttered "piercing shrieks and lamentations." This was definite drama, to be acknowledged in the fifth century by Herodotus, though he did not dare to name the theme. While these things were happening in Egypt, a theatrical performance of a very different type is recorded in the Bible as having taken place at Gaza, the "chief city of the Philistines," where Samson joined in gladiatorial games (Judges XVI, 27). A curious echo of this is the sort of show presented by and for present-day Philistines which so often baffles conscientious critics! Much richer is the life to be found in the Rig-Veda—those Sanskrit hymns which have in them the springs of true human drama. But these, at their best, came much later.

The five great empires which succeeded each other on and around the plains of Mesopotamia—the Chaldean, the Assyrian, the Babylonian, the Median, and the Persian—left nothing to inspire dramatic criticism in the time between the Egyptians and the Greeks. The Book of Job, based though it obviously is on the old Arabian folk-tale, is in its present form hardly older than the fifth century B.C. An example of the way in which apparent folk-drama has been given by priestly authority a meaning many do not attach to it is *The Song of Songs*, which proclaims itself as Solomon's. This exquisite canticle, the origin and date of which are still in dispute, must have been originally a drama, with two or more speakers. The suggestion is made in the Christian rubric that it was intended to represent not just a human love-story but the "relations of Christ to his church." This episcopal dramatic criticism is at least not essential to our delight in *The Song's* expressions of simple love. So with the old Chinese dramas, which Mr. Hsiung has adapted into *Lady Precious Stream* and *The Western Chamber*. How wisely he has retained the primitive stage-management, with realism flouted at every turn, scenes constructed before the eyes of the audience, and hundreds of miles covered in a few steps! To present-day audiences there is a comic charm about all this; but it reveals at every point the dream-like quality of drama—something that emerges from our imaginations and may be a good deal more real at the heart of it than the routine of life itself. This must have been true enough with the folk-drama of every country. How many thousand men and women of genius there must have been in the epochs before writing was devised! They may have found in the rough-and-ready play-making of their time a means of expressing to their neighbours fancies that demanded utterance—both receiving pleasure therefrom—however unrecordable the result.

Greek Theatre

With a suddenness which all the shelves of historical volumes have failed to explain came the outburst of the Greek theatre,

enriching the world with the fruits of genius for just a little
over a century and then for some reason passing off into mere
spectacle. In 535 came Thespis and his cart. One sees him
still, standing on his table and declaiming through masks to
an audience gathered on the altar-steps. In 525—just ten
years later—was born Aeschylus, even now our master in
austere tragedy. In 495—within a generation—arrived his
more human rival, Sophocles; and in 480—only fifteen years
after that—came the modern-minded Euripides, born at
Salamis on the very day of the Persian onslaught and Greek
victory. Meanwhile the theatre itself had grown into a vast
temple of dramatic art. It was at the same time a temple in
the strictest sense of the word—with an archon in management,
judges drawn by lot, and the Athenian citizens filling the
seats at two obols from early morning till nightfall. Just one
thing the Athenian theatre appears not to have had. We hear
nothing of artificial illumination. Otherwise the architects
seem to have been magicians. Even now, across a ruined
auditorium, built for 20,000, the acoustics are perfect. To
what extent did Greek criticism inspire this marvellous growth?
Unfortunately not very largely—except in the fact that every
member of the audience was an enthusiast and a critic.
Capable sometimes of violent expression, he was directly or
indirectly responsible for the judging of the plays between
authors of the standing of Aeschylus and Sophocles.

A remarkable thing is that in spite of this neither Plato in his
Symposium nor Aristotle in his *Poetic* manages to rise anywhere
near the recognition of criticism as an art. I may be grossly
unappreciative of an admitted master-writer if I confess to a
life-long disappointment over Plato's *Symposium*. This setting
of Socrates on a couch with a group of young men talking about
erotics impressed me even at school as a nasty piece of work.
It has done so ever since. As for Socrates's contribution upon
the drama—that "the same man could have the knowledge
required for writing both tragedy and comedy"—it is obviously
true sometimes, as Shakespeare long ago proved. In many
cases, on the other hand, it is utterly false. Anyhow, the contention was a waste of time. No wonder Aristophanes went to
sleep!

Aristotle

As for Aristotle, he has got the wrong idea of the art of criticism altogether. He tries to make rules, which is the prime mistake. Some of his definitions—as, for instance, that "tragedy is the imitation of an action possessing magnitude"— are sound enough. Yet, after all these centuries, we have not yet made up our minds what he means by "the purging of the soul from like passions by pity and fear." Why "like passions"? Are we to believe that no one can appreciate Oedipus who is not guilty of some repellent intrigue with a relative? My own feeling has always been that, drama being just one of Aristotle's many subjects, his practical and scientific mind was content to think of something on the face of it natural and conclusive. His rule about the unity of time was, of course, merely a costume concession to the chorus. Of this he was himself conscious. His suggestion that spectacle is "expensive" is sheer pay-sheet, and not criticism at all. His statement that it is "impious" to present a worthy man changed from prosperity to adversity, and that the sufferings of a depraved man can be neither piteous nor fearful is at once a denial of a previous rule and has a touch of priggishness completely in contrast to his main definition of tragedy. All the while there is no real, inspiring art about Aristotle's *Poetic*, no pleasing self-revelation. Here are only rules, some right and some wrong, the right ones mostly self-evident platitudes, like the need to every drama of a "beginning, a middle, and an end."

In the art of criticism not much is to be gathered from the Roman centuries. Plautus and Terence awakened no great critical mind in their immediate Roman audiences. Nor did Seneca, for all his influence upon the earlier Elizabethan dramatists, and hence upon romantic drama in general, not to mention his appearance in the Elsinore repertory. As Horace in his *Ars Poetica* warns young Piso, the tragic Muse was apt to "appear amidst wanton satyrs, like a matron bid to dance on holidays." In the great Roman theatres—Pompey's seated 40,000, or about eighteen times as many as Drury Lane—the "rich and free-born" were apt to find their good taste dominated by the "buyers of chick-peas and roasted walnuts." The adulation of Menander, in whom Plutarch found no flaw, suggests that those largely vanished plays were to some extent forerunners of our domestic and social comedies. But Rome itself was dramatically uncreative. Ovid, who had written a tragedy on the subject of Medea, without, apparently, much favourable response, charges Augustus in his *Tristia* with having, "sitting at his ease, looked upon the adulteries of the stage."

Tertullian

Then we have the attacks from the Early Fathers of the Church, typified by Tertullian's diatribes in *De Spectaculis* upon the Roman theatre's homage to "Venus and Bacchus, patrons of drunkenness and lust." St. Augustine was also stern in his rebuke of "beastliness," but more sympathetic to "genuine tragedy and comedy" as "honest and liberal studies." He had, one must remember, won a prize for a tragedy written by himself in his early Carthaginian days. The result of it all was that, after one officializing of Christianity with the Roman empire, quite apart from the excommunicating of actors by the Council of Arles in 314, spoken drama simply faded out as an entertainment in favour of chariot-races and animal fights and other excitements of the circus. One hears of efforts at tragedies on the Greek model, based on subjects taken from the Bible; but these never seem to have achieved any noticeable appeal. The people at large just fought and laboured, ate, drank, and went to the races, with pantomimes and acrobatics to amuse them in the intervals. They attended church-festivals, but did not worry their heads about dramatic art. Critics of the right kind were not there to encourage them—or, at any rate, were not sufficiently popular to do so.

CHAPTER III

ROME AND BEYOND

CURIOUSLY enough, despite the theatrical barrenness of imperial Rome there did emerge one critic whose work lives and deserves to live, though it had practically no influence on the circus-going multitude of the time. This was Longinus. In the third century he wrote a work the very name of which, *On the Sublime*, remains a standard of faith in the art he surveyed. His own Greek title meant no more than "About Height"; but in the first printed edition of 1554 this was turned into the Latin, *De Sublimitate*, which Boileau conveyed into his French version and Burke borrowed for his essay *On the Sublime and Beautiful*. The "sublime" is, it may be confessed, seldom consciously cultivated in its loftiest significance at the present day. The very word, with its still doubtful origin, is used by young people void of understanding as a synonym for ridiculous, its proverbial neighbour. Some doubt has been expressed as to whether Longinus was the true author of the work, because he does not mention any details of his remarkable career. But why should he? Does Burke bring St. James's Square or the House of Commons into his essay? Anyhow, Porphyry called Longinus "the first of critics." There is, too, something peculiarly attractive about his life—how he settled in Palmyra and became adviser in chief to that glamorous queen of the desert, Zenobia. Upon her defeat and capture he was ignominiously executed by the peasant-born Emperor Aurelian, who had no time for critics.

According to Longinus—and who would not agree?—pure sincerity is the first essential of the sublime. While avoiding all false "amplification" one should, he contends, avoid also meanness and triviality. These cannot rightly convey the kind of passion which, as we should say, "sweeps an audience off its feet." What he calls "puerility"—that is to say, pedantic imitation of masters and an assumption of a learned manner— is another thing that Longinus cannot abide. Happily the sublime is not altogether gone. There are some undoubted sublimities in T. S. Eliot's *Murder in the Cathedral*. Even Shaw, for all his evasiveness, is by no means a stranger to the sublime. Cleopatra's address to the winds of the desert; Lilith in *Back to Methuselah*; Dubedat's creed in *The Doctor's Dilemma*; Father Keegan's vision of Ireland in *John Bull's Other Island*; Lavinia's talk to the Captain in *Androcles and the Lion*—these and many other memories there are of a "great soul" speaking through every sort of mocking inhibition.

"Sakuntala"

Meanwhile, as already suggested, however little of worth-while creation was happening in Rome, the Eastern world was nurturing a drama with a magical charm about it which has never ceased—and will never cease—to haunt us. Within three or four centuries no one is still quite sure of the date of Kalidasa, the author of *Sakuntala*, though a date not long after the sack of Rome is now considered the most likely. Enough that Sir William Jones, the brilliant young Bengal judge, translated him from Sanskrit into English in 1789. This made it possible for Goethe, after reading Forester's German version, to make his classic outburst of criticism in verse—

> Wouldst thou the blossoms of spring as well as the fruits of
>   the autumn?
> Wouldst thou what charms and delights? Wouldst thou
>   what plenteously feeds?
> Wouldst thou include both heaven and earth in one
>   designation?
> All that is needed is done, when I *Sakuntala* name.

Blessings on Sir William Jones's quest and Goethe's instant and passionate recognition! It has been my good fortune to see *Sakuntala* played in all sorts of circumstances—once in the Palm House at Kew Gardens, and once on a lovely summer afternoon in the late Lord Leverhulme's garden at Hampstead, when the bright-coloured Indian silks looked for once as they were meant to look, even beneath an English sky. It has always had an exquisite beauty for me, with its delicately told idyll of King Dushyanta and Sakuntala, the woodland nymph, and of how they parted and suffered, but were made happy in the end, when the ring that had been lost was found by an old fisherman. It is very difficult to decide whether one should look upon this lovely play as very old or very young—perhaps that was what Goethe meant in his reference to spring and autumn. Charming it most certainly is.

Elsewhere in the East, too, drama was showing intellectual and spiritual vigour before this could be said of anything that was happening to a large extent west of the Bosphorus. As early as the eighth century the Chinese Emperor established in old Nanking the College of the Pear Garden, for the training of three hundred young people of both sexes in the art of the theatre. But the real makers of the Chinese drama were, of course, the Mongol emperors of the thirteenth century. We can guess what sort of drama went forward in that stately pleasure-dome which Khubla Khan decreed in his new capital of Peking. In *Lady Precious Stream*—that delicious little "Chinoiserie" to which I have already referred and which ran for two years in London—we have, on the confession of its author, an example of this. The play is, he says, an adaptation of an immemorially popular theme, of which each company that performs it in China has its own variant. It is like *Faust* or *Cinderella* with us.

The Noh Plays

One cause, possibly, of the comparative stagnation of Chinese drama after those far-off times is that, ever since Confucius, drama, like literary fiction, has been looked upon askance officially and socially. It has been different with Japan, which owes its first inspiration undoubtedly to China, but has cultivated it to far better purpose. This is betrayed especially in the Noh plays—that is to say, "plays of accomplishment." Ezra Pound writes—

> The art of illusion is at the root of the Noh. These plays, or eclogues, were made only for the few; for the nobles. . . . We find an art built upon the god-dance, an art of splendid posture, of dancing and chanting and of acting that is not mimetic. Despite the difficulties of presentation I find the words very wonderful if, as a friend says, "you read them all the time as though you were listening to music."

What Mr. Pound means may be gathered from just a few
lines in one of his own adaptations—that of a short play called
Kinuta. This proved even in an English company's performance,
as I can vouch, worthy of his praise. The story is as utterly
simple as was the setting—just a wife who has been waiting
three years for her husband. Then she dies and her ghost takes
her place—

> Sorrow is in the twigs of the duck's nest
> And in the pillow of the fishes . . .
> The voice of the pine-trees now falling
> Shall make talk in the night . . .
> We cannot see the tip of the branch.
> The last leaf falls without witness.
> There is an awe in the shadow,
> And even the moon is quiet.

I might add that in my own experience of such Chinese
and Japanese players as have appeared in London during the
past half-century I have found their acting nearly always dis-
appointing in an English theatre—the movement hampered
by the dress, the features not sufficiently expressive and
marred by the practice of squinting at moments of intensity.
On the other hand the element of dance can be, in a proper
environment, no less spiritually moving than words. The heroic
type of Noh is, of course, akin to our own Elizabethan drama—
as in the famous story of the vengeance of *The Forty-Seven Ronin*,
of which John Masefield's *The Faithful* was an adaptation.

Roswitha

Meanwhile, without any claim to a popular background, one
dramatist does gleam in the desert of European drama between
Constantine and the Crusades. This is Roswitha, the nun of
Gandersheim in Saxony. Her six plays, written in Latin
during the tenth century in imitation of Terence, still speak to
us across the ages. They tell us of a woman of genius and
learning, moved by a human sympathy which makes her
creations more alive to us now than many worldly-wise classics.
One of my most treasured memories is a production of her
Paphnutius by Edith Craig, Ellen Terry's ever-recognizant
daughter.

The story would be, in any less understanding hands, a

dreadful one—of the conversion of Thaïs, the Egyptian harlot, whom Paphnutius, the hermit, approached in the guise of a lover and converted. For me the beauty of Roswitha's original easily survives my admitted admiration for the cleverness of Anatole France's mocking treatment of part of the theme in one of his novels. The penance assigned to Thaïs in Roswitha's play was that she should be immured for five years in a cell built around her, so that there should be no escape, with a small opening through which food could be pushed. So far from this living death being a matter of sorrow to Thaïs, she is heard singing for joy as the last brick is put into its place. She lived, we are given to understand, the full five years in this seclusion, until she "being reconciled unto God by a worthy satisfaction did, after fifteen days from the completion of her penance, fall asleep in Christ." Paphnutius himself is present at this final scene. He brings the curtain down with a very beautiful prayer, holding forth a prospect of Thaïs "sharing in celestial joys" and being "set among the snow-white sheep and led into the bliss of eternity."

The real interest of it all—an interest that Anatole France misses—is the character and purpose of Roswitha herself. To what extent did she comprehend Thaïs's background and realize her atonement? Was there a Paphnutius in her case? Her abilities must have been as remarkable as her sympathies. She had already written an epic in rhymed hexameters on the Emperor Otto I. She was skilled in music, geometry, astronomy, and other arts and sciences. She was familar not only with Terence, but with Ovid, Plautus, Horace, and Virgil. But of more appeal than her learning is the note of a sincere but spiritualized passion and broad humanity that stirred her imagination. It was different from anything that had appeared in drama yet or was to appear for a very long while. What a change from the Early Fathers and their virulent and so often blundering anathemas against the art of the theatre!

Atellane Farces

Meanwhile, it is time we came back to the one form of dramatic art which is claimed to have bridged the gulf between classical and modern—the rough-and-tumble farce of the common folk. The open-air drama of the market-place has never ceased, at any rate in countries where the climate and conditions made it possible. Nearly always, sooner or later, some element of creative genius is found in these that justifies the promotion of strolling "rogues and vagabonds" to more distinguished and permanent surroundings. It happened in Attica, as we have already seen, when—

> Thespis, the first professor of our art
> To drive a trade sold ballads from a cart.

It happened in England, with the passing of drama from the inn-yard to the palace within a life-time. It happens still in the choice of kerbside troupes and concert-parties from the sands for "national" broadcasts and long-run West-End performances. It happened also, quite naturally, with the Atellane farces, brought to Rome from the little Campanian town which gave them their name. They were popular for centuries with the Roman public. They probably inspired Plautus. They were certainly demanded three hundred years later by no less critical an impressario than Petronius, the Emperor Nero's "arbiter of elegancies."

The exact details of the performance have to be imagined; but we do know that the Atellanes were originally just the mummeries of a crowd of rustic clowns. We know that they came into the theatre, like the clowns in our circuses, during the intervals of a larger spectacle. They danced, sang, made coarse jokes and obscene gestures, indulged in rough playlets on a platform especially set up in front of the stage, and finished their interlude by passing round the hat. We know, too, that the leading character of the Atellanes was Maccus, representing a cheerily depraved peasant with huge head, hooked nose, and double hump. In him there is no possible reason why we should not recognize a prototype of the future Neapolitan Pulcinella and, in spite of doubters, a forfather of our own Mr. Punch. Then came Pappus, perhaps just an early and rude version of the Venetian pantaloon. With them were the clown, Stupidus, the infamous parasite, and the gobbling Bucco. All these and the other Sanniones, or "zanies," were buffoons to start with.

So, though the idea is discredited in some quarters, began the *Commedia dell' Arte*—the famous Italian "professional comedy" which was to come to flower so remarkably in the sixteenth century, lingering still in our own Punch and Judy, and in Pierrot and Columbine and what is left of the panto-mime-harlequinade.

CHAPTER IV

MEDIEVAL DRAMA

STRANGE as it might seem from some points of view, though it was really logical enough, the rebirth of the drama in medieval times was to come, broadly as well as individually, through the Church which had suppressed it. Roswitha was not alone. Of all the plays which the Middle Ages gave us there is at least one which combines in an almost miraculous degree exactly the qualities that Longinus demanded in the sublime—simplicity, dignity, and sincerity of manner. I mean, of course, *Everyman*, that tragic masterpiece, "purging the soul" as surely as any of Aristotle's favourites, and yet utterly without pomp or pretentiousness and spoken in language to be equally understood by prince and pauper. An obvious piece of clerical propaganda, it breaks through all the trammels of its class with a quality of dramatic creation which marks out its unknown author as a man of genius. It was not printed until 1529, the year in which Sir Thomas More became Henry VIII's Chancellor. No one knows whether the English or later-published Dutch version was made first; but both go back to the parable of three friends in Balaam and Jehoshaphat, written by the Patriarch of Antioch over four centuries before. This, in its turn, is from a Buddhist source.

"Everyman"

The history of *Everyman* upon our modern stage deserves a reference here as showing how, in face of the true sublime, age and language and even creed have no power to destroy dramatic values. I happen to have seen the old play in practically every form, including the late William Poel's "discovery" of it for modern purposes at the Charterhouse. It was done then in the open air, with Everyman going down into an actual grave. Round it sparrows hopped and twittered. This enhanced the stark and gripping truth of the message that, when all have gone from Everyman—friends, kindred,

wealth, beauty, strength, and even the "Five Wittes"—Good
Deeds alone can survive the last ordeal.

After that unforgettable performance, the late Sir Philip
Ben Greet took over *Everyman* from William Poel. Year
after year, on both sides of the Atlantic, Sir Philip presented
the play with a good taste and understanding which never
failed. These were more than ever in evidence on the occasion
of Sir Philip's last revival, when the Bishop of London, deeply
stirred by the performance, came forward at the finish to
express his gratitude. Other productions have not been so
exemplary. The temptation always is to elaborate *Everyman*
into a pageant, as Reinhardt did with Hoffmansthal's version
at Salzburg—not to mention others in this country. All
credit for the best *Everyman* tradition is due to the creative
imagination of William Poel. His original studies of the various
characters set a standard to all since that has never been
improved upon. The single personage of Everyman; Death,
conceived and acted by Poel himself in a spirit of grisly comedy,
with his harsh, high-pitched, peremptory summons falling
ruthlessly on Everyman's ear; the clamorous jollity of Friendship and Kindred; the calm dignity of Knowledge—all these
were given by Poel, and by Greet after him, a living, individual
character that nothing has yet effaced.

Moralities

The vogue of moralities which made *Everyman* possible
grew—so we are made to believe by Sir Edmund Chambers—
out of allegorical scenes in the miracle-plays, the study of
which by critics, dramatists, and producers, has been so inspiring
and fruitful during the past hundred years. How much had
happened between Roswitha's timid effort at a sacred Terence
in the tenth century and the outcoming of *Everyman* in its
printed form in the sixteenth! Denied a legitimate drama, the
lay world had, for the better part of a millennium, to rely for
entertainment upon minstrels of one sort or another. It is
well to keep in mind that "minstrel" originally meant only a
minor servant, without any necessary connexion with music
or any other art. Nor were the early minstrels, as entertainers,
by any means always the equivalent of the Court poets and

troubadours to whom romance has accustomed us. They
included hosts of tumblers, rope-walkers, conjurers, puppet-
masters, animal-impersonators, and other quite uncreative
performers. These corresponded, as nearly as changing time
allows, to the familiar turns of a modern variety programme.

To what extent did the very large profession thus created
welcome the Church's return to an interest in the stage with the
establishment of public miracle-plays and mysteries? This
point could be further studied with advantage, in spite of the
literature which has grown up round the miracle-plays themselves, of which the moralities were a late off-shoot. The
miracle-plays seem to have emerged from their place in the
liturgy to become a public and popular institution in England
with the Corpus Christi processions outside the church in the
fourteenth century. How they came to be transferred to the
craftsmen's guilds under municipal management in towns like
York and Coventry, and to semi-religious organizations like
that of the Parish Clerks at Clerkenwell has not yet been traced
quite as clearly as one might wish. All seem to be agreed
that the word "mystery" has nothing to do—in England at
any rate—with the other "mystery," which implies secrecy
and is from the same root as "mute" and "mum." The
mystery-play is, apparently, like "minstrel," akin to "ministry,"
i.e. service. But the kind of service meant is still an affair of
academic controversy. It may refer to the craft or "mystery"
of the skilled workers who presented the play, or to the liturgy
of the Church, from which the play originally sprang, or to the
"Fraternities of Corpus Christi," who saw to payment, or to a
guild of the actors themselves. But of any such guild we hear
nothing further, save for the "royal guild of minstrels," founded
by Edward IV in 1469—and the word "mystery" was in use
half a century before then. On the other hand, there were
earlier "courts of minstrelsy," which claimed to issue licences
to all performers.

It is a pity that more is not known about this first arrival
of the actors as an organized profession since the days when the
Church had suppressed the theatres. Through all the time
between, Sir Edmund suggests, the actors had been "absorbed
into that vast body of nomad entertainers on whom so much

of the gaiety of the Middle Ages depended." They had "padded the hoof along the roads in little companies of two and three, travelling from gathering to gathering, making their own welcome in castle or tavern or, if need be, sleeping beneath a wayside hedge in the white moonlight."

Miracle-plays

Undoubtedly the miracle-plays were largely acted by the priests themselves, as is suggested in the vivid, if unsympathetic, description found by Hone in an old black-letter volume called *The Beehive of the Romish Church*—

> Christ hath not done anything in His death and Passion, but they do plaie and counterfeite the same after him, so trimlie and livelie that no plaier nor juggler is able to doe it better. . . . I speak not of their perambulations, processions, and going about the town, carrying their crucifixes along the streets, and there play and counterfeite the whole Passion, so trimlie with all the Seven Sorrows of Our Lady as though it had been nothing else but a simple and plain enterlude.

Needless to say, there were two sides to this as to every question. The Wycliffite author of a fourteenth-century sermon quoted in Wright and Halliwell's *Reliquiae Antiquae* takes, for instance, a distinctly different point of view. He writes—

> Summe recreatioun men moten han, and bettere it is, or less yvele, that they han theyre recreatioun by pleyinge of myraclys than by pleyinge of other japis. Also, sithen it is leveful to han the myraclis of God peynted, why is it not as well leveful to han the myraclis of God pleyed, sythen men mowen bettere reden the wille of God and his mervelous werkis in the pleyinge of hem than in the peyntinge, and bettere thei ben holden in mennus mynde and oftere rehersid by the pleyinge of hem than by the peyntinge, for this is a deed bok, the tother a quick.

With or without opposition, the miracle-play became in the end a thoroughly official affair. The Corporation of York issued a proclamation for the control of street traffic during the performances at each "station" round the town at which the pageant-cars, drawn by horses, stopped in turn. Here is Archdeacon Rogers's description of the Whitsun plays at Chester in 1594—

> Every company had his pagiant or parte, which pagiants weare a high scaffolde with two rowmes, a higher and a lower,

upon four wheeles. In the lower they apparelled themselves, and in the high rowme they played, being all open on the tope, that all behoulders might see and heare them. The places where they played them was in every streete. They begane first at the abaye gates, and when the first pagiante was played it was wheeled to the Highe Crosse before the Mayor, and so to every streete.

It is a far cry from the derided simplicities of *The Beehive* to these elaborate spectacles of York and Coventry and Chester. Sometimes the pageant-cars were three-decked, with a lower floor for hell-fire and an upper for God and the angels. According to a proclamation in the municipal records of York for 1476, four of the "most connyng, discrete and able players within this city" were called before the Mayor to—

serche, here and examen all the plaiers and plaies and pagentes. And all such as they shall find sufficient in personne and connyng, to the honour of the citie, and worship of the saide craftes, to admitte; and all other insufficient personnes, either in connyng, voice or personne to discharge, ammove and avoide.

Professionals

All this prompts a certain curiosity as to the arrival of the professional actor, and how far it caused, or was caused by, the transfer of management from the Church to the town. It would be well to know, too, if it happened before or after, or coincided with, the use of the pageant-car. We know that the performers were paid. A Coventry record sets down 3s. 4d. to the impersonator of God, who had to gild his face, and 8d. to a sort of utility man, Fawston by name. His fee included 4d. for "hangyng Judas" and 4d. more for "coc croyng." According to Chambers, "there is nothing to show that the performers were drawn from the minstrel class. They were probably members of the guilds undertaking the plays."

Altogether it is clear that much critical research might yet be done on this question of the reappearance of the professional actor. Very many things go to hint at a certain continuity right through the Middle Ages. We know that Shakespeare may have seen the actual Coventry play, as it continued to be performed until 1580, when he was sixteen, and Stratford on Avon is only a few miles away. We know also that the miracle-play traditions were part of the lore of the professional stage of his day—for example, Hamlet's allusion to "o'er-doing Termagant" and "out-Heroding Herod." At the same time, the repertory of the "comedians of the city" who arrived at Elsinore included Plautus and Seneca, and an evidently exhaustive bevy of tragical-pastoral-comical productions, with "scene indivisible and poem unlimited." In France and elsewhere in Europe the miracle-play reached a comparatively high development much earlier than it did here. This was so beyond doubt, if one may judge by the austerely simple yet beautiful *The Play of Adam and Eve*, written in the twelfth century. It was acted some years ago, under the direction of M. Gustave Cohen, in modernized French at the Sorbonne and, later, on the steps of Chartres Cathedral. In this there is none of the concession to popular taste which characterizes the English miracle-plays—though Satan was probably a grotesque demon. Nor is there any of the display of nudity which Warton claimed for the Garden of Eden in English guise. *The Play of Adam and Eve* has still much of the quality of a liturgical solemnity. M. Cohen himself says—

> By its psychological subtlety and metaphysical elevation, *The Play of Adam and Eve* satisfies the critical. At the same time the despair of Adam and Eve finds its way to every heart, and brings tears to the eyes by its sincerity when acted with the requisite skill. . . . This symbolic drama—is it not still that of our human destiny, ever swinging between far-off hopes of eternity and the immediate joys of earthly life?

"Robin and Marion"

No less valuable has been M. Cohen's production of the thirteenth-century pastoral play, *Robin and Marion*, presented in the same year, with a company of students from the Sorbonne, at University College, London. This medieval operette —one of the loveliest things imaginable—was the composition of Adam le Bossu de la Halle. It brings back to us, as no modern romantic imitation could do, the days of the trouvères. Childlike in its innocence, it yet reveals a more deplorable state of social affairs than *The Beggar's Opera* itself. Marion, a shepherdess, is shown in imminent danger of being carried off from her forest-home by a violent knight, who comes

riding by with a falcon at his wrist. Robin, her shepherd
swain, is completely overcome by a social inferiority-complex in
facing the knight. Indeed, if it had not been for Marion's
faithfulness, he would never have seen her again. But, when
Marion has thrown herself from the knight's horse and returned,
and a wolf threatens her pet lamb, Robin drives off this new
intruder unaided and without a tremor. With the knight
and the big bad wolf both disposed of, Robin and Marion
and the other shepherds and shepherdesses settle down to
fun and games, including country-dances, cross-questions and
crooked answers, and other party-romps, finishing up in a
merry jamboree, with garlands for everybody and Marion
queen of the feast. I have told the story just to show how little
some things—and how much others—have altered in the
seven hundred years that have passed since this fragrant and
rollicking old medley was first presented, probably beneath
a castle wall, with bright eyes glancing from the battlements.

"The Marvellous History of St. Bernard"

A more sophisticated but none the less delightful old French
play, blending chivalry with sanctity and touching its theme
with the imaginative grace of true romance, is *The Marvellous
History of St. Bernard*. This was presented by Sir Barry Jackson
in 1926 at the old Kingsway Theatre, in English. It has been
translated by himself from M. Henri Ghéon's version of a
fifteenth-century manuscript—the only one in existence—
belonging to the Comte de Menthon. The play tells of St.
Bernard de Menthon's early life as a young noble of the
tenth century, his prospective marriage, his flight from home,
and his vision of the Blessed Virgin. One of the characters is
that of the medieval jester, forerunner of Feste and Touchstone
and other "dear fools of Shakespeare." Indeed, the whole
play has a special appeal as lying between the devotional and
the romantic. Thanks to Ghéon and Sir Barry, it preserves
the charm of both.

Interludes

Another kind of play, or, rather, another word for almost
all kinds of play, makes its appearance with the eve of the

Renaissance. This is the interlude. It covers almost every sort of performance, grave and gay, short and long, public and private, from Plautine farce to heavy morality. Even the meaning of the name is still undecided. It obviously denotes a "play between"; but whether it is between people or events is a question still to be answered. Through this very vagueness of outline the interlude was able to cover almost all that lay between the miracle-play and morality and the full-fledged drama and romantic comedy of the Elizabethans. It perpetuated much, including the comic "Vice" of the moralities, who held to his ancient coxcomb and charter of waggery. In the main it may be taken to mean a performance given at Court, in the royal presence at Whitehall or Greenwich, or at the Inns of Court, or at college festivities at Oxford or Cambridge, or at Eton or Westminster School, as against a popular show in the street.

On its original production, Nicholas Udall's adaptation of Plautus's *Miles Gloriosus* into *Ralph Roister Doister*, the first English comedy—whether it was during his headmastership of Eton or of Westminster—was described as an "interlude." So was *Gammer Gurton's Needle*, when it was presented before Queen Elizabeth at Christ's College on her visit to Cambridge in 1564. Not less so had been the presentation two years before of Sackville and Norton's *Gorboduc*, the first blank-verse tragedy to be seen upon an English stage, at the Inner Temple Christmas revels. We have to thank John Heywood, Henry VIII's "player of the virginals," for the gradual development of the interlude as a distinct species of light, short, professional play for festal performance, distinguished from the danced masque, or "disguising," in which the royal personages themselves took part.

Several of his interludes well repay production even now. I was present at a performance, given by Miss Ruby Ginner, of Heywood's pleasantly imaginative frolic, *The Play of the Wether*. This most happily combines the purposes of a morality and a satire, with its story of how Merry Report, the comedian or "Vice," introduces to Jupiter all sorts of people who want different weather. The gentleman wants dry weather for hunting, the merchant good winds for sailing, the forester,

the water-miller, the wind-miller, the gentlewoman, and the
laundress all want something different. Finally a small boy
wants "plenty of snow to make my snow-balls." Jupiter
settles the matter by promising to give all of them the weather
they want in turn—an arrangement which would serve, now
as then, to explain away the troubles of our English climate.

Revival

Apart from *Gorboduc* I happen to have seen all these interludes and comedies—not forgetting Medwall's fifteenth-
century *Fulgens and Lucres*, the earliest of them all. They have
been played, and very well played, either in London or in
provincial theatres before delighted audiences. The revival
of what one may call the medieval spirit in drama is a notable
sign of the dramatic life of our time. It is a case not merely
of rummaging in museums, but of entering into the very
soul of the feudal world. It is having its creative influence.
The miracle-plays, themselves lovingly represented in church
as well as in playhouses and the open air, have found intimate
modern echoes in such varied forms as M. André Obey's *Noé*
and Mr. Charles Claye's *A Joyous Pageant of the Holy Nativity*.
Everyman itself has been challenged by modern spiritual
allegories like *Eager Heart*. Both the pastoral and the early
romantic drama have been exploited, as we have seen, with
beautiful results. It is singular that Sir Walter Scott, whose
interest in the life and industry of the folk was in some circumstances hardly less strong than his love of chivalry, has little
that is happy to say about medieval drama. He entirely
fails to appreciate the naïve sincerity and racy humours of
the English miracle-plays—

> The poetic value of these mysteries is never considerable. It
> was soon discovered that the purity of the Christian religion was
> inconsistent with these rude games, in which passages from
> Scripture were profanely and indecently mingled with human
> inventions of a very rude and sometimes indecorous character.

As against the dead indifference of Scott and his theatrical
contemporaries, one finds nowadays a revitalization of the
drama of the folk in every kind, from folk-dance to passion
play. This may be partly due to a consciousness of social

changes everywhere, and the threatened extinction of all sorts of beliefs and customs in a mechanical age. But it shows at the same time a desire for something that mechanism cannot give—elemental humanity, with which the drama is essentially and eternally concerned. They are by no means only awakenings of the past, these revivals of old ideals, fancies, conventions. They are often inspirations for the future. To help in recognizing and furthering them is one of the genuine values of dramatic criticism, whether in theatre, library, or village hall.

CHAPTER V

ELIZABETHAN AWAKENING

AS some cicerone upon a future liner of the outer spaces might be imagined saying, when the machine suddenly melts and its passengers frizzle, "We are now approaching the sun." It is of no use to make pretences about other times and other places. Shakespeare and the Elizabethans were and are a solar system of the drama, outshining anything within telescopic vision. Though the shelves of whole libraries groan with critical works upon the Elizabethan output, we are too near Shakespeare even now not to be dazzled. People who are quite sane about everything else just lose their heads when they come to Shakespeare. A librarian once said to me, in surveying his Shakespearian section: "Every book here has a bee in its bonnet."

He was very nearly right. For some the miracle of Shakespeare can be explained only by the nonsensical process of making it a greater miracle still. So we have the "Baconians" and the "Oxfordians." Every play has inspired some wild theory. The chief reason is that, while there are all sorts of easy explanations for the form and faults and technique of Shakespeare, there is none for his creative genius. It has just to be taken for granted, like the origin of all energy. If one does this it is astonishing how easily everything else fits in, and how little need exists for those unfortunate obsessions which have led the minds of some of our ablest scholars astray. Supposing Shakespeare had been the normal product even of his glorious age, he would arrive just as the best exponent of the romantic drama, a natural product of the Renaissance, carrying on the tradition begun by Marlowe. A distinguished attempt to "place" him thus was made by John Addington Symonds in his *Mermaid* essay—

> Shakespeare's work can be regarded as the expansion, rectification and artistic ennoblement of the type fixed by Marlowe's epoch-making tragedies. In very little more than fifty years

from the publication of *Tamburlaine*, our drama had run its
course of unparalleled energy and splendour. Expanding like
a many-petalled flower of marvellous complexity and varied
colours, it developed to the utmost every form of which the
romantic species is capable, and left to Europe a mass of work
invariably vivid, though extremely unequal, over which, of course,
the genius of Shakespeare rules supreme. He stands alone and
has no second; but without the multifarious excellencies of
Jonson, Webster, Heywood, Beaumont, Fletcher, Ford, Massinger
and a score whom it would be tedious to enumerate, the student
would have to regard Shakespeare as an inexplicable prodigy.

"Pawle's Crosse"

Here we have the needless trouble of so many critics succinctly
put. Their snag is the dread of permitting an "inexplicable
prodigy" to exist whereas, in our practical and still more in
our spiritual lives, we accept a host of "inexplicable prodigies"
quite cheerily. The simple fact is that Shakespeare lives
because we love him. On the other hand, however "explic-
able" they may be—indeed, just because they are so—who
wants to worry about the "multifarious excellencies" of a
score of dead names which even their champion finds "tedious
to enumerate"?

The beginnings of Elizabethan criticism are, it must be
confessed, not encouraging. No sooner were the elder Burbage's original Theatre and the Curtain established "without
the liberties" at Shoreditch, than criticism began. It began,
where it had triumphantly and disastrously ended over a
thousand years before, with the clergy. The first mention of
the London theatres occurs in a sermon preached at "Pawle's
Crosse" by the Rev. T. Wilcocke on 3rd November, 1577,
"in the time of the Plague"—

> Looke upon the common playes in London, and see the multi-
> tude that flocketh to them and followeth them. Beholde the
> sumptuous theatre-houses, a continual monument of London's
> prodigalitie and folly. But I understande they are now forbidden
> because of the plague. I like the pollicie well if it holde still, for
> a disease is but bodged or patched up that is not cured in the
> cause, and the cause of plagues is sinne, if you look to it well;
> and the cause of sinne are playes: therefore the cause of plagues
> are playes.

John Stockwood, schoolmaster of Tonbridge, preaching soon after from the same pulpit, was more picturesque if not so logical—

> Wyll not a fylthye playe, wyth the blast of a trumpette, sooner call thither a thousande, than an houre's tolling of a bell bring to the sermon a hundred? . . . Why should I speake of beastlye playes, against which every man out of this place cryeth out? Have we not houses of purpose built with great charges for the maintenance of them, and that without the liberties, as who should saye: "There, let them saye what they will saye, we will playe." . . . For, reckoning with the leaste, the gaine that is reaped of eight ordinarie places in the Citie which I knowe, by playing but once a weeke (whereas many times they play twice and sometimes thrice) it amounteth to 2,000 pounds by the yeare.

This kind of thing was all the encouragement that the elder Burbage and his colleagues had towards giving the public something better than they wanted at the time when Shakespeare, as a boy of 14, was still "creeping like snail unwillingly to school" at Stratford on Avon.

Gosson's "Schoole of Abuse"

In the following year, 1579, arrived the first effort at anything like intelligent dramatic criticism printed in English. This was Stephen Gosson's *Schoole of Abuse*. It is described on its title-page as containing "a pleasant invective against Poets, Pipers, Plaiers, Jesters and suchlike Caterpillars of a Commonwealth, setting up a Flagge of Defiance to their mischievous exercise, and overthrowing their Bulwarkes, by Prophane Writers, Natural Reason, and common experience." Outwardly a mere reckless diatribe, this work of a young Oxonian, who had been himself an actor as well as a dramatist, some of whose plays were yet to be produced, is on a much higher plane than anything recorded of the pulpiteers. Whatever his grievance was, Gosson knew what he was talking about. He is out to entertain at all costs. Like many modern critics—known in stage-parlance as "knockers"—he imagines that the best way to achieve this is by violent attack, enriched by choice allusions, racy anecdotes, and supposedly sensational revelations. In a word he was a journalist of his period, not

of the best type, but brilliant in his own kind. His description
of the audience, for instance, though ostensibly framed to
shock the reader, is in reality a very lively and attractive
piece of writing, done with evident relish and calculated, if
anything, to add to the crowd whose numbers and manners
it effects to deplore—

> In our assemblies at playes in London, you shall see such
> heaving and shoving, such ytching and shouldring, to sitte by
> women; Such care for their garments, that they be not trode on;
> Such eyes to their lappes that no chippes light in them; Such
> pillowes to their backes that they take no hurte; Such masking
> in their eares, I know not what; Such giving them pippins to
> pass the time; Such playing at foot Saunt without Cardes;
> Such ticking, such toying, such smiling, such winking, and such
> manning them home when the sportes are ended, that it is a
> right Comedie to mark their behaviour.

When it comes to the plays, the only ones that he mentions
are those that he praises, one of them anticipating Marlowe's
The Jew of Malta and Shakespeare's *The Merchant of Venice*, and
others of his own, about the merits of which he is at least not
diffident. The yard of the old Belle Sauvage Inn on Ludgate
Hill, where performances were given, is still to be traced. The
Bull was in Bishopsgate Street—

> The two prose bookes plaied at the Belsavage, where you shall
> finde never a woorde without wit, never a line without pith,
> never a letter placed in vaine. *The Jew* and *Ptolome*, showne at
> the Bull, the one representing the greedinesse of worldly chusers,
> and bloody mindes of Usurers: the other, very lively, descrybing
> how seditious estates with their own devises, false friendes, with
> their own swoordes, and rebellious commons with their own
> snares, are overthrown; neither with amorous gesture wounding
> the eye; nor with slovenly talk hurting the ears of chast hearers.
> *The Blacksmith's Daughter* and *Catilin's Conspiracies* usually brought
> in to the Theater; The first containing the trechery of the
> Turkes, the honourable bounty of a noble mind, and the shining
> of vertue in distresse. The last because it is known to be a pig of
> myne own sowe, I will speake the lesse of it. . . . These playes
> are good playes and sweete playes, and of all playes the best
> playes and most to be liked, woorthy to be soung of the Muses, or
> set out with the cunning of Roscius himself. . . . Now, if any
> man aske me why myselfe have penned comedyes in time paste
> and inveigh so eagerly against them here, let him know I have
> sinned and am sorry for my own fault. Hee runs far that never

turns. Better late than never. I gave myself to that exercise in hope to thrive, but I burnt one candle to seek another, and lost both my time and my travell, when I had done.

Sidney's "Apologie"

While it is not without value in itself, one merit of Gosson's *Abuse* is that it drew an answer from Sir Philip Sidney, to whom it was dedicated. According to Edmund Spenser, in "dedicating it to Maister Sidney," Gosson was for his labour "scorned, if at least it be in the goodness of that nature to scorn." Anyhow, Sidney took four years to think out his response in *The Apologie for Poetry*. In so far as they deal with drama, the "sacred, pen-breathing words of divine Sir Philip Sidney," as Olney's foreword calls them, prove singularly behind the times. As will be seen in the following extract, he fusses about the supposed "laws" of Aristotle, unaware of the outburst of romantic genius which was soon to scatter them to the winds—

Our tragedies and comedies (not without cause cried out against) observe rules neither of honest civility nor of skilful poetry. . . . For where the stage should always represent one place, and the uttermost time presupposed in it should be, by Aristotles precept and common reason, one day; there is both many days and many places inartificially imagined. You shall have Asia of the one side and Afric of the other, and so many under-kingdoms that the player, when he cometh in, must ever begin with telling where he is, or else the tale will not be conceived. Now ye shall have three ladies walk to gather flowers, and then we must believe the stage to be a garden. By and by we hear news of shipwreck in the same place, and then we are to blame if we accept it not for a rock. Upon the back of that comes out a hideous monster, with fire and smoke, and then the miserable beholders are bound to take it for a cave. In the meantime, two armies fly in, represented with four swords and bucklers, and then what hard heart will not receive it for a pitched field? . . .

Besides these gross absurdities, how all their plays be neither right tragedies nor right comedies, mingling kings and clowns, not because the matter so carrieth it, but thrust in clowns by head and shoulders to play a part in majestical matters with neither decency nor discretion. . . . Our comedians think there is no delight without laughter, which is very wrong.

The great fault even in that point of laughter, and forbidden plainly by Aristotle, is that they stir laughter in sinful things, which are rather execrable than ridiculous, or in miserable, which are rather to be pitied than scorned. For what is it to make folks gape at a wretched beggar or a beggarly clown, or, against the laws of hospitality, to jest at strangers, because they speak not English so well as we do?

Much of this discourse might prompt in our day the exclamation: "Elementary, my dear Sidney!" But it has to be remembered that Sidney was writing of romantic drama before it had rightly begun to exist in this country. All was still crude and chaotic as against the fully formed classic models. He could not be expected to see what was coming, and he did not do so. At the same time his criticism is well worth recalling. It does not represent merely the assertion of second-hand "laws." It is an expression, to some extent, of his genuine character and of a serious interest in the stage, even if his preference was for dull echoes of Seneca or grisly themes, like that of *Gorboduc*, from British mythology.

Gosson's View

It is clear from Gosson and the preachers that the popular theatres were at least doing varied and vigorous work in dramatic production. Tragedies and chronicle-plays as well as comedies were already affording a higher alternative to bear-baiting and acrobatics; though practically all the plays which were to make the Elizabethan stage famous were yet to be written. Gosson himself declared that: "*The Palace of Pleasure, The Golden Ass, The Aethiopian History, Amadis of France* and *The Round Table* have been thoroughly raked to furnish the playhouses in London."

In the circumstances it means something that so elegant and gravely-disposed a courtier as Sidney should have frequented the public theatres at all at that time. If they were in the least like Gosson's description of them they were hardly the place for the Earl of Leicester's idolized nephew. But Sidney's allusions to crude "clowning," and "scurrility," and "doltishness," and poverty of display hardly suggest that he confined his attentions to Court or private performances. The "jewel of knighthood" was to meet his death on the battlefield

at Zutphen two years later, without knowing the glory that
was to come to the theatre which he had, in principle, set out
to defend. Gosson, meanwhile, went into the Church. He
was for twenty years rector of St. Botolph's, Bishopsgate, and
died in 1624, in his seventieth year.

"Tamburlaine"

It was just a couple of years after Sidney's death that Marlowe's *Tamburlaine the Great*, recently seen in London with
Donald Wolfit in the title-part, was first presented, and a
newly created Elizabethan drama sprang into splendid being.
Inevitably "Marlowe's mighty line" has stirred critics to noble
prose. Here is the tribute paid by Dr. Frederick Boas, author
of *Shakespeare and His Predecessors*, and the leading authority
on Marlowe, in a particularly well-considered study—

> In the stupendous career of this Oriental conqueror the young
> poet saw a subject exactly suited to his purpose. Such heroical
> deeds of arms fittingly set forth upon the stage would put to
> shame the buffooneries of the popular plays. Accordingly he
> threw into the creation of *Tamburlaine* the full, ardent force
> and passion of his genius. The result was a mighty, Titanic
> figure, throbbing with intense vitality, a figure that, by sheer
> masterful pressure, storms its way into the imagination. It is
> in its highest aspects an embodiment of its author, and of the
> epoch which he supremely represents. A distinguishing note of
> the Renaissance age, intoxicated by the magnificent possibilities
> opened to it on every side, was an uncontrollable aspiration
> after the ideal, a scorn of earthly conditions, a soaring passion
> that sought to scale the infinitudes of power, beauty, thought, and
> love. It is this spirit, ever one and the same, that breathes in
> Sir Thomas More's vision of a perfect society, in Spenser's
> pattern of the highest, holiest manhood, in Bacon's clarion-call
> to the conquest of "all knowledge" and in the heroic deeds and
> speeches of Sidney, Gilbert and Greville. But nowhere does it
> find more characteristic vent than in Marlowe's *Tamburlaine*,
> though it there takes chiefly yet not solely, its least noble form—
> the thirst for limitless power.

As a constructive dramatist Marlowe does not come off so
well. Even Swinburne, in treating of *Tamburlaine*, speaks of
"the stormy monotony of Titanic truculence, which blusters
like a simoom through the noisy course of its ten fierce acts."
Over *Doctor Faustus* impassioned praise has to be set off against

even more apology. Goethe's curiously inappropriate exclamation, "How greatly it is all planned!" is adroitly excused by Dr. Boas, who suggests that: "the play is conceived on noble lines, and the beginning and the end are worthily executed; but between them there is a yawning gap."

Upon all these views it is a remarkable comment of modern fact that Marlowe's *Doctor Faustus* was, not many years ago, one of the big successes of the Federal Theatre in America. Possibly everybody is right. After all, Marlowe is always aided by his own fiercely imaginative quality—not least in the ironic agonies of *Edward II*. But, in his earlier plays, at any rate, he had not learnt, or troubled about, anything that we should call comprehensive dramatic construction. He was primarily and always a rhetorical poet, passionate infidel, and Machiavellian apostle, with far too strong a personality and purpose to create convincing characters detached from his own temperament. But as poet his immortality is secure. He stood, as Chapman put it, "up to the chin in the Pierian flood," and Drayton's lines will be for ever true which tell us that—

> Marlowe, bathed in the Thespian springs,
> Had in him those brave translunary things
> That our first poets had: his raptures were
> All air and fire, which made his verses clear:
> For that fine madness still did he retain,
> Which rightly should possess a poet's brain.

Kyd's "The Spanish Tragedy"

Of Shakespeare's other predecessors not much need be said here. Their value to our living drama lies mainly in Shakespeare's debt to them, so that they are really part of his saga. We have had several productions during the past twenty years or so of Kyd's *The Spanish Tragedy*. It is full of interest for museum purposes, presenting as it does the germ of the play-scene in *Hamlet*. One may note that Kyd is still first favourite for being probable author of the original Hamlet-play itself, with the gloating over revenge. This, of course, Shakespeare turned back-to-front in its appeal and made his own. Like *Hamlet*, too, *The Spanish Tragedy* follows the Seneca tradition of bringing in a ghost. It dabbles in every sort of

horror and drowns the stage in blood. Undoubtedly the play
was an enormous favourite with a then comparatively untu-
tored public, which revelled in gore. Burbage, we know,
played with success as "old Hieronimo," the Spanish father
who avenges the murder of his son. He arranges a play-scene,
which ends in a cluster of actual stabbings. Afterwards the
father bites out his tongue and adds his own to a heap of other
corpses. It suggests by contrast what Shakespeare rose from,
not what he means to us. No critic has made his fame by
expressing from his innermost heart a joy in Kyd's *The Spanish
Tragedy*. It is just a question of research and half-hearted
praise, with a due assortment of "ifs" and "buts," on the part
of scholars like Dr. Boas and Sir Edmund Chambers, to whose
admirable works all students may be readily referred. But
it is not this kind of thing which makes dramatic criticism
worth while.

Far more modernly sympathetic and not less important to
the making of Shakespeare were the Court pastorals of John
Lyly, the author of *Euphues*. Born in 1553, and coming down
from Magdalen College, Oxford, he was the eldest of the
"University wits" destined to be beaten by Shakespeare at
their own game. Though Shakespeare did inevitably "our
Lyly outshine"—together with "sportive Kyd and Marlowe's
mighty line—the inventor of "euphuism" does not seem himself to have resented the coming of his brilliant disciple. At
the same time it is difficult not to feel a certain sympathy over
Robert Greene's famous allusion in his *A Groat's-worth of Wit,
bought with a Million of Repentance*—

> There is an upstart crowe, beautified with our feathers, that
> with "Tyrgre's heart wrapt in a player's hide" supposes he is as
> well able to bombaste out a Blanke Verse as the best of you;
> and, being an absolute Johannes fac-totum is, in his own conceyt,
> the only Shake-scene in a country.

Lyly's "Campaspe"

Poor Greene was evidently referring to Shakespeare's share
in *Henry VI*, where the "tiger's-heart" line occurs, and to the
young actor-playwright's easy skill in heroics. But it was the
style of Lyly, the "euphuistic" elegance of the Court pastoral,

that was to characterize Shakespeare's first original play, *Love's Labour's Lost*. Shakespeare's genius was to use and develop and humanize this to his own purpose just as it was to use and develop and humanize the blank-verse "bombast." It is possible that Lyly, just ten years Shakespeare's senior, and Greene and Peele, who were respectively four and six years older than the Warwickshire intruder, have not even now had full critical justice done them. Lyly's *Campaspe*, telling of the rivalry between Alexander the Great and the painter Apelles for the favour of Campaspe, the fair Theban, with Diogenes and other philosophers intervening, has some delightful writing in it. The "euphuistic" wit is concocted, to be sure, according to a simple Sitwellian recipe, upon which Shakespeare was to improve at every point. Alliteration, antithesis, and fantastic allusion become rather tedious as a repeated pattern. One can have too much embroidery, also, of any kind. But Queen Elizabeth may have been in leisurely mood on the New Year's night of 1584, when *Campaspe* was played at Court by "Her Majesty's children and the children of St. Paul's." *Alexander and Campaspe* was its full title.

Whether the more general audience at the Blackfriars theatre, where it was repeated, enjoyed it so well there is no knowing. It contains at any rate one song which has achieved something like immortality in "Cupid and my Campaspe," and hosts of happy images. As the writer of a best-selling novel as well as of comedies that reached the private ear of the Queen with approval, Lyly seems to have been comparatively fortunate. He was more so, at any rate, than his fellow-Oxonian, Peele, and than Greene, who was at both Oxford and Cambridge. Though he failed to induce Queen Elizabeth to appoint him Master of the Revels, Lyly was able to join Lord Burghley's household in a more or less dignified capacity and survived the century.

Arcades Ambo

Meanwhile, both Greene and Peele had ended lives of dissipation with early and miserable deaths. Yet there are graces in Peele's *The Arraignment of Paris*, another Court production, and a pastoral freshness and truth about the country-scenes in Greene's *Friar Bacon and Friar Bungay*, which at least herald the coming of the master not of one style but of all. Some personal qualities also that deserved a better end must have been discernible in both, to judge by Thomas Nash's preface to Greene's *Menaphon* in 1589, and his reference there to Peele—

> I dare commend him to all that know him as the chiefe supporter of pleasance now living, the Atlas of Poetrie and *primus verborum artifex*, whose first encrease, *The Arraignment of Paris*, might plead to your opinions his pregnant dexteritie of wit and manifold varietie of invention wherein (*me judice*) hee goeth a step beyond all that write. Sundrie other sweete Gentlemen I know, that have vaunted their pens in private devices and trickt up a companie of taffata fooles with their feathers, whose beauties if our Poetes had not peecte with the supply of their periwigs, they might have antickt it untill this time up and downe the country with the King of Fairie and dined every day at the pease-porridge ordinary.

The fact that Greene had anticipated Shakespeare by bringing Oberon into a play about James IV of Scotland, and that the occasion and date of the first performance of *A Midsummer Night's Dream* are still unknown, may or may not have some bearing upon the question as to who one of those "sweete Gentlemen" was!

CHAPTER VI

CRITICS AND SHAKESPEARE

NOW to the problem of suggesting within anything like reasonable limits the critical reaction to Shakespeare himself. An enormous mass of theory and analysis and the critical treatment of particular plays will have necessarily to go by the board, at any rate for the time being. I am going to take for granted that the author of the plays was William Shakespeare from Stratford on Avon, though there is no possible reason against accepting just as much external inspiration and collaboration as may seem to have been likely at the time and in the circumstances.

One pleasantly simplifying fact is that first and last the solvent of all needless discussion is the man himself, as revealed both by the plays and poems and by what is known of the life of Shakespeare. There is, at the heart of it, no difference between the opinion of his contemporaries and the latest and most enlightened criticism. When once we bring ourselves to take the technical supremacy of Shakespeare for granted, and to think of him as a man, we find that it is really by his human qualities, not by the intellectual machinery of his work, that he remains unapproached in his universality of appeal to all classes of all nations who have the means of knowing him. We find that this was the outstanding view of those who knew him in life. Both they and the most penetrating critics since have taken, as it were, two shots at estimating Shakespeare.

"Friendly Shakespeare"

One is a long-distance shot. It generally results in mere dazzlement at his miraculous gift of language and its music, his skill as a dramatist, and his imaginative power as a poet and as a creator of some two thousand distinct characters. This estimate tends to get rather pompous and useless nowadays, when Shakespeare's supremacy in each direction has for so long ceased to be news. Some who study him closer find that it is, after all, the man who matters, the universal sympathy of one to whom friendship was the most important thing in life. We know that a feeling of this dual aspect of Shakespeare was in evidence quite early during his career. Before the final *Hamlet*, or *Macbeth*, or *Othello*, or *King Lear* was produced, Francis Meres was writing in his *Wit's Treasury* (1598)—

> As the soule of Euphorbus was thought to live in Pythagoras; so the sweete, witty soule of Ovid lives in mellifluous and honey-tongued Shakespeare, witness his *Venus and Adonis*, his *Lucrece*, his sugared sonnets among his private friends. . . . As Plautus and Seneca are accounted the best for Comedy and Tragedy among the Latins; so Shakespeare among the English is most excellent in both kinds for the stage.

It was an even more exalted paragon of whom Anthony Scoloker wrote in *Daiphantus* (1604)—

> Like friendly Shakespeare's tragedies, where the comedian rides, while the tragedian stands on tiptoe.

Of the friendliness of Shakespeare what more perfect proof than the testimony of his fellow-players, Heminge and Condell, editors of the First Folio?—

> We have but . . . done an office to the dead, to procure his Orphanes, Guardians; without ambition either of self-profit or fame; onely to keepe the memory of so worthy a Friend and Fellow alive as was our Shakespeare . . . who, as he was a happie imitator of Nature, was a most gentle expresser of it. His mind and hand went together: And what he thought he uttered with that easiness, that we have scarce received from him a blot in his papers.

Ben Jonson

No one, of course, combines the two views better than Ben Jonson. On the one side is the splendour of his First Folio tribute to "the memory of my beloved, the Author, Mr. William Shakespeare"—

> Soul of the Age!
> The applause! delight! the wonder of our Stage!
> My Shakespeare, rise; I will not lodge thee by
> Chaucer or Spenser, or bid Beaumont lye
> A little further to make thee a roome;
> Thou art a Monument without a tombe . . .

> Triumph, my Britaine, thou hast one to showe,
> To whom all scenes of Europe homage owe.
> He was not of an age, but for all time!
> And all the Muses still were in their prime,
> When like Apollo he came forth to warme
> Our eares, or like a Mercury to charme . . . .

Then, twelve years after, we find Jonson writing in his *Discoveries—*

> I remember the players have often mentioned it as an honour to Shakespeare that in his writing (whatsoever he penned) he never blotted out a line. My answer hath been, "Would he had blotted out a thousand!" which they thought a malevolent speech. I had not told posterity this, but for their ignorance who chose that circumstance to commend their friend by wherein he most faulted and to justify mine own candour. For I loved the man, and do honour his memory, on this side idolatry, as much as any. He was, indeed, honest and of an open and free nature; had an excellent phantasy, brave notions and gentle expressions, wherein he flowed with that facility that sometimes it was necessary he should be stopped. . . . His wit was in his own power; would the rule of it had been so, too! Many times he fell into those things that could not escape laughter; as when he said, in the person of Caesar, one speaking to him, "Caesar, thou dost me wrong!" he replied "Caesar did never wrong without just cause"; and such like—which were ridiculous.

Milton

Whether or no "rare Ben" had just cause in this—the passage, as quoted, does not occur in any known edition of the play—a sense of Shakespeare's friendliness is clear enough. Another double view is that of Milton. On the one hand we have with the Second Folio his majestic epitaph, written in 1630, fourteen years after Shakespeare's death, and marred only by the weak tautology of "wonder and astonishment" in the seventh line—

> What needs my Shakespeare for his honoured bones,
> The labours of an Age in piled stones,
> Or that his hallowed Reliques should be hid
> Under a star-ypointing pyramid?
> Dear Sonne of Memory, great Heire of Fame,
> What needst thou such weak witness of thy Name?
> Thou in our wonder and astonishment
> Hast built thyselfe a lasting Monument.

But, when he was off the heroic vein, in "*L'Allegro*" (1632),
we have something far more intimate—

> Or sweetest Shakespeare, fancy's child,
> Warble his native wood-notes wild.

Some three years later, old Thomas Heywood, who must
have been speaking from personal memory, writes in his
Hierarchie of the Blessed Angels—

> Mellifluous Shakespeare, whose enchanting quill
> Commanded Mirth or Passion, was but will.

What pleasant touches, too, are those of John Aubrey, who,
though he was not born until nine years after Shakespeare had
died, knew more about him than many who were his contemporaries!—

> This William . . . began early to make essays at dramatic
> poetry, which at that time was very low; and his plays took well.
> He was a handsome, well-shaped man, very good company, and
> of a very ready and pleasant, smooth wit. . . . I have heard
> Sir William Davenant and Mr. Thomas Shadwell—who is
> accounted the best comedian we have now—say that he had a
> most prodigious wit, and they did admire his natural parts beyond
> all other dramatic writers.

Dryden and Pope

With the Restoration, and right on through the eighteenth
century, criticism went awry in both, or rather all, directions.
It exaggerated homage on the one hand to boring deification.
It degraded friendliness on the other to the assumption that
Shakespeare, who "breathed books" and, like the much
lowlier-born Carlyle, drank in knowledge at every pore, must
have been an ignorant boor, just because he was taunted by
Jonson with having "small Latin and less Greek." Hence the
Baconian theory and all sorts of troubles, though Jonson's
phrase would equally apply to Shaw, Pinero, Jones, H. G.
Wells, and also to Noel Coward, St. John Ervine, and countless
brilliant people of our day. The fashion was set by Dryden.
While substituting his own wretched travesty for *The Tempest* on
the assumption that Shakespeare was an inspired idiot who
did not know his own job, he apologizes for his great original
in specious wise—

> Those who accuse him to have wanted learning, give him the

greater commendation. He was naturally learned. He needed not the spectacles of books to read nature—he looked inwards and found her there. I cannot say he is everywhere alike. Were he so I should do him an injury to compare him with the greatest of mankind. He is many times flat and insipid, his comic wit degenerating into clenches, his serious swelling into bombast. But he is always great when some great occasion is presented to him. No man can say he ever had a fit subject for his wit, and did not then raise himself as high above the rest of poets. . . . In him we find all arts and sciences, all moral and natural philosophy, without knowing that he ever studied them.

In prefacing his own edition of the plays, Pope carries on the baleful tradition of wondering patronage—

His sentiments are not only in general the most pertinent and judicious on every subject, but by a talent very peculiar—something between penetration and felicity—he hits on that particular point on which the bent of each argument turns or the force of each motive depends. This is perfectly amazing from a man of no education or experience in those great and public scenes of life, which are usually the subject of his thoughts; so that he seems to have known the world by intuition, to have looked through human nature at one glance and to be the only author that gives ground for a very new opinion, that the philosopher and even the man of the world may be born as well as the poet. It must be owned that, with all these great excellencies, he has almost as great defects; and that as he has certainly written better, so he has, perhaps, written worse, than any other.

How comes it that an editor of Shakespeare could charge the alderman's son from Stratford's quite reputable grammar-school, a protégé of Southampton before all the greater plays were written, and soon, as the Lord Chamberlain's own dramatist, intimate with every detail of the life of Queen Elizabeth's Court, with being "a man of no education or experience in public scenes of life"? From this "yokel" standpoint, the most unutterable bathos ever written about Shakespeare was surely that of Gray's *The Progress of Poesy*—

In thy green lap was Nature's darling laid
What time, where lucid Avon strayed,
To him the mighty mother did unveil
Her awful face; the dauntless child
Stretched forth his little hand, and smiled.
"This pencil take," she said, "whose colours clear

Richly paint the vernal year:
Thine too, these golden keys, immortal boy!
This can unlock the gates of Joy,
Of Horror that, and thrilling Fears,
Or ope the sacred source of sympathetic Tears."

Samuel Pepys

Meanwhile irresponsible playgoers may have been pardoned for looking upon the garbled verse, mechanical toys, and wig-and-plume displays that went for Shakespeare from the Restoration onwards with a mixture of bewilderment and boredom. Even in the days of Betterton, Samuel Pepys, that eager first-nighter, has hardly a good word to say for any Shakespearian production—except *Macbeth*. This he saw in the more or less operatic version arranged by Davenant, with a good many of the finest lines mangled beyond recognition, and any amount of gaudy mechanical spectacle. He paid five recorded visits to the play at the Duke's, or Duke of York's Theatre, in Lincoln's Inn Fields. Some of his remarks are not so trivial as others. At least we know they were genuine, and were made to please nobody but himself—a kind of criticism which can be as valuable as it is rare. Here are some of his entries—

Nov. 5, 1664. To the Duke's House to see *Macbeth*, a pretty good play, but admirably acted.

Dec. 28, 1666. To the Duke's House, and there saw *Macbeth* most excellently acted, and a most excellent play for variety.

Jan. 7, 1667. To the Duke's House and saw *Macbeth*, which, though I saw it lately, yet appears a most excellent play in all respects, but especially in divertisement, though it be a deep tragedy; which is a strange perfection in a tragedy, it being most proper here and suitable.

Oct. 16, 1667. To the Duke's House, and I was vexed to see Young, who is but a bad actor at best, act Macbeth, in the room of Betterton, who—poor man!—is sick.

Dec. 21, 1668. To the Duke's House, and saw *Macbeth*. The King and Queen there, and we sat just under them and my Lady Castlemaine. . . . Lady Castlemaine, when she saw Moll Davis, looked like fire.

Amidst distractions of this order, and with the kind of treatment bestowed by the producers of the period, it was hardly Shakespeare's fault that Pepys registered *A Midsummer Night's Dream*

as "the most insipid, ridiculous play that ever I saw in my life."
He found *Henry VIII* to be "so simple a thing, made up of a
great many patches, that, besides the shows and processions in
it, there is nothing in the world good or well done." He "ever
heretofore esteemed *Othello* a mighty good play, but having so
lately read *The Adventures of Five Hours*, it seems a mean thing."
As for *The Merry Wives of Windsor*, it "did not please me at all,
in no part of it." He had a slightly better opinion of Dryden's
and Davenant's debased version of *The Tempest*, which he saw
on its first night and describes as "an old play of Shakespeare's"—

> The house was mighty full, the King and Court there; and
> the most innocent play that ever I saw; and a curious piece of
> musick in an echo of half-sentences, the echo repeating the former
> half, while the man goes on with the latter; which is mighty pretty.
> The play has no great wit, but yet is good above ordinary plays.

"The Spectator"

Happily—thanks to Heminge and Condell, and to Nicholas
Rowe, and some succeeding editors—these travesties could not
put out of count the real Shakespeare, submerged though he
was for nearly a hundred years so far as the stage was concerned.
If Quin, whose "right hand knew not what his left hand did,"
looked anything like his portraits as Coriolanus when he
appeared in Tate's version of Shakespeare's play, one feels that
the shade of Shakespeare must have been glad that his original
was temporarily suspended. Even Addison contents himself
with a glimpse of Shakespeare as a kind of Puck peeping in
from the moonlight upon the dreary fustian of the contemporary
stage. There Addison's own *Cato*, now laden with the dust of
two centuries, was considered an exciting work. The best
The Spectator had to say about Shakespeare is this—

> There is a kind of writing, wherein the poet quite loses sight of
> Nature, and entertains his reader's imagination with the charac-
> ters and actions of such persons as have, many of them, no exis-
> tence, but what he bestows upon them. This Mr. Dryden calls
> "the fairy way of writing". . . . Among all the poets of this
> kind Shakespeare has incomparably excelled all others. That
> noble extravagance of fancy which he had in so great perfection,
> thoroughly qualified him to touch this weak, superstitious part
> of his reader's imagination; and made him capable of succeeding,
> where he had nothing to support him besides the strength of his

own genius. There is something so wild and yet so solemn in the speeches of his ghosts, fairies, witches and the like imaginary persons, that we cannot forbear thinking them natural, though we have no rule by which to judge of them, and must confess, if there are such beings in the world, it looks highly probable that they should talk and act as he has represented them.

Voltaire

It was Voltaire's curiously Shavian blend of ferocious and utterly unfair attack, with a suggestion of grudged appreciation, that woke up criticism on this side of the Channel to values in Shakespeare hitherto ignored or looked upon as deficiencies. Voltaire's three years in England undoubtedly left him with a very keen and shrewd idea of what was good in the English character and constitution, and also in our national dramatist. But praise was not Voltaire's hobby, and his first interest was himself. So he cribbed everything he could for his own plays and gave his "discovery" the tang of controversy, so useful for publicity purposes, by mixing his assertions up with virulent abuse. This use of "punch" is an old trick of a game in which Voltaire—the inventor of the *claque*—knew every move. Here is the celebrated bombshell in a letter prefacing his own *Semiramis*—

> *Hamlet* is a gross and barbarous piece, and would never be borne by the lowest rabble in France or Italy. Hamlet runs mad in the second act and his mistress in the third; the prince kills the father of his mistress and fancies he is killing a rat; and the heroine of the play throws herself into the river. They dig her grave on the stage, and the gravediggers, holding the dead men's skulls in their hands, talk nonsense worthy of them. Hamlet answers their abominable stuff by some whimsies not less disgusting; during this time one of the actors makes the conquest of Poland. Hamlet, his mother, and father-in-law, drink together on the stage. They sing at table, quarrel, beat and kill one another. One would think the whole piece was the product of the imagination of a drunken savage. And yet, among all these gross irregularities, which make the English theatre even at this day so absurd and barbarous, we find in *Hamlet*, which is still more strange and unaccountable, some sublime strokes worthy of the greatest genius. It seems as if nature took pleasure to unite in the head of Shakespeare all that we can imagine great and forcible, together with all that the grossest dullness could produce of everything that is most low and detestable.

Dr. Johnson's Answer

This was a direct pull at the tail of the British lion, which responded with a roar from an altogether appropriate quarter. Dr. Johnson's preface to his edition of Shakespeare (1765)— though his own predilections had been hitherto all in favour of the classic unities and pompous artifice—stands out as a sturdy, if reluctant, essay in championship. It rehearses most of the things common sense could find to say on Shakespeare's behalf at that time. Johnson did not mind reproving Shakespeare as if he were a naughty child, and patronizing him extensively (particularly in his notes), but from Voltaire he will accept no ruling—

> This is the praise of Shakespeare, that his drama is the mirror of life; that he who has mazed his imagination in following the phantoms which other writers raise up before him, may here be cured of his delirious ecstasies by reading human sentiments in human language, by scenes from which a hermit may estimate the transactions of the world, and a confessor predict the progress of the passions. His adherence to general nature has exposed him to the censure of criticks, who form their judgments upon narrower principles. . . . Voltaire censures his kings as not completely royal. Dennis (the author of *An Essay on the Genius and Writings of Shakespeare*, 1712) is offended that Menenius, a senator of Rome, should play the buffoon; and Voltaire perhaps thinks decency violated when the Danish usurper is represented as a drunkard.
>
> But Shakespeare always makes nature predominate over accident; and if he preserves the essential character, is not very careful of distinctions superinduced and adventitious. His story requires Romans or kings, but he thinks only on men. He knew that Rome, like every other city, had men of all dispositions; and wanting a buffoon, he went into the senate-house for that which the senate-house could certainly have afforded him. He was inclined to show an usurper and a murderer not only odious but despicable; he therefore added drunkenness to his other qualities, knowing that kings love like other men, and that wine exerts its natural power upon kings. These are the petty cavils of petty minds; a poet overlooks the casual distinction of country and condition, as a painter, satisfied with the figure, neglects the drapery.

The Unities

One need not follow Johnson in his ponderous but effective arguments against the tryanny of the unities of time and place, where romantic drama is concerned. The whole controversy is now as dead as a door-nail. The wonder is that it should have raged so long, and that the supposed authority of Aristotle, in "laws" which Aristotle never laid down, should have definitely hindered the development of the drama in France. Then, as now, the law of necessity was quite stringent enough. A too-frequent change of place is inadvisable still—not because it destroys illusion, but because in a scenic production it costs more, which Aristotle would have regretted, and leads to long waits or lumbering mechanics. A single-set comedy will always have an advantage in the eyes of an economical manager. But why there should have been so much fuss about something that Aristotle did not say, and about the need for excusing the presence of a chorus that had long vanished, is one of the still-unexplained curiosities of criticism.

Certainly Johnson, against his earlier judgment, trained his gun quite formidably upon the battlements of that fortress of false tradition. His loyalty to Shakespeare is less sure. He will always pick a hole where he can. Some of his "asides" have an element of justice in them—as, for instance, this on Shakespearean "quibbles," though the "euphuism" in which Shakespeare's wit was schooled was partly to blame—

> A quibble is to Shakespeare what luminous vapour is to the traveller; he follows it at all adventures; it is sure to lead him out of the way and sure to engulf him in the mire. It has some malignant power over his mind and its fascinations are irresistible.

One pronouncement of Johnson's may be regarded as deplorable from every point of view. It is—

> Not one of Shakespeare's plays, if it were now exhibited as the work of a contemporary writer, would be heard to the conclusion.

This may well have been so in Johnson's time. The fault was simply the bad taste of the public. But, with all he undoubtedly did to bring the eighteenth-century world nearer to an appreciation of Shakespeare, one cannot help feeling that Johnson was never a whole-hearted "Shakespearian." Even his famous verse-tribute, with its laborious epigrams, is a remote half-satirical homage—

> When Learning's triumph o'er her barbarous foes
> First reared the stage, immortal Shakespeare rose.

> Each change of many-coloured life he drew,
> Exhausted worlds and then imagined new;
> Existence saw him spurn her bounded reign
> And panting Time toiled after him in vain.

Goethe and Lessing

While Johnson's *Shakespeare* was going through its early editions, and "brave old Samuel" himself had still eight years to live, an entirely new orientation was being taken towards Shakespeare by a young man of 21, who was studying law and writing poetry at Strasbourg. The young man was Goethe. No one can describe better than himself the effect Shakespeare had upon him. What a complete change is his whole attitude from the self-satisfied apologies for Shakespeare's ignorance, and surprise at his knowledge, which had hitherto done duty for critical communion! This was the way genius greeted genius in 1775—

> Do not expect me to write much or to write sedately; tranquillity of soul is no garment for a festival; and even still I have thought little about Shakespeare; to divine him, feel him in great passages, is the highest to which I have been able to attain. The first page I read in him made me his for life, and when I had reached the end of the first play, I stood like one born blind, on whom in a moment a miraculous hand had bestowed sight. I recognized, I felt most intensely, that my being had been infinitely widened; everything was new to me, unknown, and the unwonted light gave me pain in my eyes. Gradually I learned to see, and, thanks to my receptive nature, I still feel intensely how much I have gained.

It may be admitted that Lessing deserves the credit for being Shakespeare's earliest critical sponsor in Germany. He had already shown characteristic insight and initiative in accepting Shakespeare's defiance of the unities as against the French classicists who had hitherto dominated the German stage. But Goethe's response was something quite fresh. The sense of intimacy and revelation to which he confesses was the arrival of a new understanding, a new criticism, of Shakespeare and his magic. It is the first suggestion of a true sympathy with the man revealed in the plays. It is the first recognition that his characters are not merely reflexes either of the Elizabethan and earlier world or of our own, but an extension of both.

They are creations just as real, speaking a language of musical rhythm which is their own and none other's, but beguiling us with laughter and tears as readily as if they were our close companions. This point of view was to be very beautifully put by De Quincey in his *Biographical Essay*—

> Shakespeare has extended the domains of human consciousness, and pushed its dark frontiers into regions not so much as dimly described or even suspected before his time, far less illuminated (as they now are) by beauty and tropical luxuriance of life. For instance—a single instance, indeed, one which is in itself a world of new revelation—the possible beauty of female character had not been seen as in a dream before Shakespeare called into perfect life the radiant shapes of Desdemona, of Imogen, of Hermione, of Perdita, of Miranda and many others. The Una of Spenser, earlier by ten years than most of these, was an idealized portrait of female innocence and virgin purity, but too shadowy for a dramatic reality. As to the Grecian classics, let not the reader imagine that any prototype in this field of Shakespearean power can be looked for there.

Schlegel

After Goethe, it is to Schlegel's *Lectures on Dramatic Art and Literature*, delivered in Vienna and translated into English in the year of Waterloo, that we owe the restoring in England—quite apart from their effect in Germany—of undimmed enthusiasm for Shakespeare. Both Coleridge and Hazlitt confessedly owe their inspiration to Schlegel, whom Hazlitt quotes in full by way of preface to his own *Characters of Shakespeare's Plays*. It was Schlegel's privilege to remind Shakespeare's countrymen of their own dramatist's mastery of passion as well as of character—

> This tragical Titan, who storms the heavens, and threatens to tear the world from off its hinges; who, more terrible than Aeschylus, makes our hair stand on end, and congeals our blood with horror, possessed, at the same time, the insinuating loveliness of the sweetest poetry. He plays with love like a child, and his songs are breathed out like melted sighs. He unites in his genius the utmost elevation and the utmost depth; and the most foreign, and even apparently irreconcilable properties subsist in him peaceably together. The world of spirits and nature have laid all their treasures at his feet. In strength a demigod, in profundity of view a prophet, in all-seeing wisdom a protecting

spirit of a higher order, he lowers himself to mortals, as if unconscious of his superiority, and is as open and unassuming as a child.

All this seems a little tumid for these days. But one has to remember that it coincided with Byron and the Napoleonic aftermath. Our stage, and to some extent that of Germany as well, was given over to the spectral and the sentimental. Kotzebue and "Monk" Lewis were favoured authors at our patent theatres. Mrs. Siddons was retiring and Edmund Kean making his first appearance at Drury Lane. It was a time when both critics and dramatists thought it a good thing to dip their pens in earthquake and eclipse.

Leigh Hunt

If one wants a study of Shakespeare from which the shadows are missed out altogether, one may find it very charmingly done by a critic of just the same period. Leigh Hunt had the happy faculty of forgetting all troubles, public and private, when he could gather a nosegay of fancies. Here is his view of Shakespeare expressed in *The Indicator*, 3rd May, 1820—

> O thou divine human creature—greater name than even divine poet or divine philosopher—and yet thou wast all three!—a very spring and vernal abundance is to be found in thy productions! They are truly a second nature. We walk in them with whatever society we please; either with men or fair women or circling spirits, or with none but the whispering airs and leaves. . . . The tears which thou fetchest down are like the rains of April, softening the times that come after them. Thy smiles are those of the month of love, the more blessed and universal for the tears.

This might be described as Shakespeare "up to the pretty," but it does not take into account *Titus Andronicus*, *Timon of Athens*, and *Troilus and Cressida*. It does not answer for the greater tragedies that grapple with life's agonies, explore the madhouse and the sepulchre, but still leave us with a sense of faith not lost.

Coleridge and Hazlitt

Neither Coleridge nor Hazlitt is quite satisfactory as a guide to Shakespeare, though they both deal at length with the structure of the plays, and Hazlitt with the acting of them as well. Both impress upon us the universality and reality of Shakespeare's characters—as, indeed, does every critic of importance. But, when it comes to the man himself, Coleridge buries his head in philosophic sand, and Hazlitt leaves Schlegel to "carry on." Coleridge's very tough essay in *The Friend* on "The Principle of Method" reduces it all to a kind of natural system. What he exactly means is not too easy to discern, beyond the obvious fact that Shakespeare's characters live differently, though he is behind them all and their life-blood comes from him. Coleridge says—

> We find individuality everywhere; mere portrait nowhere. In all his various characters we still find ourselves communing with the same nature which is everywhere present as the vegetable sap in the branches, sprays, leaves, buds, blossoms and fruits, their shapes, tastes and colours. . . . We may define the excellence of their method as consisting in that just proportion, that union and interpenetration of the universal and the particular, which must ever pervade all works of decided genius and true science.

Bernard Shaw

By way of contrast—and yet, in one important particular, remarkable agreement—we may turn direct from these strangely humourless visionaries of the Regency to a great critic-dramatist who, though he has now passed away, can still be claimed to belong to our own time, Bernard Shaw. In his notice in *The Saturday Review* of the revival of *Cymbeline* at the Lyceum in 1896, Shaw wrote—

> There are moments when one asks despairingly why our stage should ever have been cursed with this "immortal" pilferer of other men's stories and ideas, with his monstrous rhetorical fustian, his unbearable platitudes, his pretentious reduction of the subtlest problems of life to commonplaces, against which a Polytechnic debating-club would revolt, his incredible unsuggestiveness, his sententious combination of ready reflection with complete intellectual sterility, and his consequent incapacity for getting out of the depth of even the most ignorant audience, except when he solemnly says something so transcendently platitudinous that his more humble-minded hearers cannot bring themselves to believe that so great a man really meant to talk like their grandmothers. . . .
> But I am bound to add that I pity the man who cannot enjoy

Shakespeare. . . .   His gift of telling a story (provided someone
else told it to him first); his enormous power over language, as
conspicuous in his senseless and silly abuse of it as in his miracles
of expression; his humour; his sense of idiosyncratic character;
and his prodigious fund of that vital energy which is, it seems,
the true differentiating property behind the faculties, good, bad,
or indifferent, of the man of genius, enable him to entertain us
so effectively that the imaginary scenes and people he has created
become more real to us than our actual life—at least until our
knowledge and grip of actual life begins to deepen and glow
beyond the common.   When I was twenty I knew everyone in
Shakespeare, from Hamlet to Abhorson, much more intimately
than I knew my living contemporaries.

Shakespeare's Self

Taking all due discount from Shaw's playful "artillery
preparation," it may be noticed that, like Coleridge and De
Quincey, he found the characters of Shakespeare more real
than those of actual life. He also, like Goethe, experienced the
peculiar appeal that Shakespeare has to young minds, which
kindle like torches at the touch of Shakespeare's sympathy with
them.   Clearly there must be something more than "vital
energy" behind this—some ideal world which opens to the
imagination more convincingly than Leigh Hunt's pretty
picture or Schlegel's miraculous blend of sublimity and horror.

My own conviction is that only by the study of Shakespeare's
—the Stratford Shakespeare's—actual life and plays together
can we get at a right sense of what he means to us of this
present time. In spite of his supreme power as a creative artist
one may still find in the plays that magnetic personality which
reveals itself through them. It is magnetic not only because
it is well expressed, but because it was in itself a rare and
beautiful personality. In speaking of the man, Shakespeare,
we must think not merely of the Shakespeare of legal and paro-
chial records, though they help, but of the ideal Shakespeare.
With us all there is a truer self than any register can show—
a self which exists not in the accidents of fortune, but in the
ideals we believe in and which we convey to others.

If we search out this Shakespeare we find that he was by
no means just an Elizabethan. In spite of his popularity, he
was at many points against the spirit of that adventurous but

at the same time treacherous and pedantic era. To his contemporaries the doctrines of Machiavelli still appealed as a desirable basis of conduct. Death by torture, brutal amusements, and flagrant immorality were commonplaces. The idea that Shakespeare's magic was due to his being a "child of his age" is very much overdone. Great things were undoubtedly happening then; but we have definite evidence that the world was every bit as full of stupid, dull, priggish, deceitful, mean, and generally repulsive people in Queen Elizabeth I's reign as it is to-day—if not more so.

Order of Ideals

The ideals that Shakespeare stood for—the things he was keen about, in his order of emphasis—show him to have been very much out of the common style, whether of his day or of ours. As I have already suggested, the chief of these ideals was friendship. It was with Shakespeare not merely something useful and to be cultivated on that account, but a profound passion. We know from the Sonnets, whatever their true history may be, what friendship meant to Shakespeare. Some equable souls, Sir Sidney Lee among them, have looked upon these heart-cries as fantastic exaggerations. Not so others. Disraeli, of all people, used not only to uphold Shakespeare's view of friendship, but confessed that his own experience confirmed it. It was Shakespeare's primal and persistent theme. Hamlet wore Horatio "in his heart's core." The quarrel-scene between Brutus and Cassius has a personal note which would speak to us just as poignantly if neither Caesar nor the Roman Republic had ever existed. Both *The Merchant of Venice* and *Much Ado About Nothing* are comedies of friendship triumphant. Yet Shakespeare's faith in friendship was peculiarly against the spirit of his time, rife as that was with public and private treachery, from the Throne downwards.

Young Love

Another ideal of Shakespeare's which was by no means shared by all his contemporaries was that of young and innocent love. Among all dramatists he was, and is, its supreme champion. Though he ranged "from hell to hell" of human passions

5—(G.412)

he never lost this ideal. He carried it right through from the Biron and Rosaline of his first play to the Ferdinand and Miranda of his last—youth and faith, brought together by Prospero's art over trackless continents and uncharted seas. Shakespeare did more than believe in the inspiring power of young love. He gave it a language which expresses the feelings natural to young people and at the same time ennobles them. He makes youth's wondering hopes and sensitive imaginings articulate. In these days, when the popular bookshelf, the stage, the picture-theatre, the radio, and some newspapers are largely reservoirs of weak sentiment and sordid cynicism, the strength and beauty of this one ideal in Shakespeare would in itself answer for much of the passionate homage he evokes.

I remember vividly making a special visit to the sixpenny gallery at the Lyceum during the late Ernest Carpenter's Shakespearian revivals at popular prices in 1908. I wanted to see to what extent Shakespeare's language was understood by a supposedly uneducated public. The play was *Romeo and Juliet*, with Matheson Lang and Norah Kerin in the title-parts. The gallery was crowded with young people of the industrial class. They had not yet learned American from the film and had practically no language to express their intimate emotions, except Cockney monosyllables of a debasing sort. But there was no doubt about their understanding of Shakespeare. They were spell-bound—

> Sleep dwell upon thine eyes; peace in thy breast;
> Would I were sleep and peace, so sweet to rest!

Not a single word is there, one may notice, unknown to the lowest standard of vocabulary. The emotion is one common to every physically healthy young man and woman. But no one in that old Lyceum gallery could mistake the revelation of Shakespeare's power to give spiritual beauty to what would otherwise be despised and coarsened.

Then came the burning flame of his patriotism; his love of country life and its sports, of horses, of pastoral folk, of flowers; his reverence for music and knowledge of it; his rich and never sneering humour; his keen interest in scientific discoveries; his belief in the dignity of business—a belief for which he has been contemptuously stigmatized as "middle-class," though it is difficult to see what he had to be ashamed of in this; his faith in manhood and womanhood; his ultimate radiant optimism of a "brave, new world," where Ariel is set free. All these things are true alike of the Shakespeare of the plays and of the Shakespeare who came from Stratford to London, suffered, struggled, won through, went back to his lovely country home, and died there an honoured land-owner and lay-rector.

Personal Revelation

This "personal-to-Shakespeare" view goes far to account for the magnetism which just puzzled the critics of other generations. It has been enormously helped by the labours of editors and researchers of the past seventy or eighty years. Professor Dowden's *Shakespeare: His Mind and Art* (1875) was a pioneer work in this respect. Our debt is also incalculable to Dr. F. J. Furnivall's discoveries as to the order of the plays and their dates. Let Dr. Furnivall, who was my indomitable old friend and master, explain the reason in his own characteristic and lively way, as he did when introducing *The Royal Shakespeare* (1894)—

> I believe that all the deepest and greatest work of an artist is based on personal experience. Shakespeare tells me he's felt hell, and in his Othello, Macbeth, Lear, Coriolanus, Timon, I see the evidence of his having done so. He tells me how he loved his friend, as with woman's love; and in his Antonio—thrice repeated—his Helena, his Viola, I see his own devoted love reflected. He tells me what his false, swarthy mistress was; and in his Cleopatra I see her, to some extent, embodied. Tradition tells me of the merry meetings at the Mermaid, and the wit-combats there; and in the Falstaff scenes at the Boar's Head I see these imaged.

Not only in the externals which Dr. Furnivall described so simply and so vividly does Shakespeare's self-revelation in his characters endear them to us. It may be doubted, for example, if Falstaff would ever have seized upon mankind's imagination as he has done if he had been only an echo and vision of someone heard and seen "at the Mermaid." Is not the immortal part of him an element that is Shakespeare's own? He was, after all, not only the world's greatest jester, but an embodied and, in the end, pathetic assertion of the fallacy that "life is a jest." I believe that this was no mere outward observation with Shakespeare, but something deeply wrought in with his personal history. It lends an intimate truth to all those "dear fools" of his. I believe that he had it in his blood and owed it, as Dickens owed Micawber, to his own father, the Stratford alderman, who was a "merry-cheeked old man" and, as we know, came to grief.

Hamlet and Falstaff

As it has a bearing upon Shakespeare's ideals, I may, perhaps, be pardoned for quoting from a comparison of Hamlet with Falstaff which I contributed, by request, to the Frankfurt *Römerberg festschrift*—

The kinship of Falstaff and Hamlet has often been noted, as in Tree's version of Falstaff's soliloquy upon "Honour," spoken in Hamlet's manner. Both of them represent the ultimate failure in practical life of that form of madness called "artistic temperament." It was a failure of the danger of which in himself Shakespeare was keenly conscious. He emphasizes it in his Sonnets—

'Tis true I have been here and there,
And made myself a motley to the view,
Gored mine own thoughts, sold cheap what is most dear.

Hamlet was the artist in tragedy; Falstaff the artist in comedy. Both saw life not as a reality but as a play. Hamlet wanted to dramatize the killing of Claudius instead of doing it; Falstaff sacrificed everything to win laughter by comic adventure or bright retort. His was the tragedy of being a comedian. Both of them are contrasted with men who, without a tithe of their wit or intelligence, keep a practical purpose always in view. What Fortinbras and Laertes are to Hamlet, Prince Henry and Hotspur are, in the realm of comedy, to Falstaff. Many critics who should have known better have been puzzled by Prince Henry's opening confession of distrust in Falstaff's escapades, his early determination to throw off loose behaviour before long, and his disowning of Falstaff at the finish. But these are definitely in the character of the practical organizer, with that shrewd eye to the main purpose which Falstaff and Hamlet lacked. Prince Henry is no less Shakespeare's ideal of a courageous and responsible commander for being a bit of a prig—everyone who has to pretend to be better than his fellows must be that. Nor need Falstaff be the less himself for representing almost everything that

a "hero" should not be. Shakespeare had potentially all Falstaff's
waywardness as well as his wit; but in practical affairs, after
early slips, he was able to borrow something at any rate, of his
own Henry's wisdom.

Bacon and Oxford

One reason for the especial value of the closer love and knowledge of Shakespeare brought by the study of his life at Stratford and in London is that it does afford a check to the weed-
growth of the "Baconian," "Oxfordian," and other theories.
Ludicrous in itself to anyone who even considers the style of
the two men, the idea that "Bacon wrote Shakespeare" is now
nearly a century old. It has thrived, partly on its sheer
nonsensicality, ever since Miss Delia Bacon published her
book, *The Philosophy of the Plays of Shakespeare Unfolded* (1857).
She died a lunatic two years later. In 1887 a new impulse was
given, also from America, by Ignatius Donnelly's publication of
The Great Cryptogram, and again in 1900 by Mrs. Gallup's
The Bi-Literal Cipher of Francis Bacon. Though these have nothing
whatever to do with the spirit of Shakespeare, they have
fascinated what one may call the jig-saw puzzle element—a
very large one—in the public mind. They have also stimulated
the study of Bacon. The cipher itself has had some valuable
fruits from the point of view of code-telegraphy and otherwise.
The Bacon Society, to pursue further Baconian investigations,
was founded in 1885. Its annual dinner has seldom failed to
provide fresh entertainment in the shape of some new and wild
theory. It has now long been mooted that Bacon was the son
of Queen Elizabeth, and the few doggerel versions of the
Psalms which are his poetic legacy have fostered a suggestion
that credits him with the entire Authorized Version of the
Bible. In the face of speculations of this kind, the comparatively modest Bacon-Shakespeare theory has, in itself, rather
dwindled of late.

Those who are now on the look-out for a puzzle-author to
the plays mostly favour Edward de Vere, the seventeenth
Earl of Oxford, a theory put forward in *Shakespeare Identified*
by T. Looney (1920). The sixth Earl of Derby and third
Earl of Rutland are candidates chosen by French students,
A. Lefranc (1919) and C. Demblon (1913), respectively. It

remains probable that Shakespeare, like most great creative workers, absorbed ideas from every available source. Among his influential friends there may easily have been one who "nightly gulled him with intelligence." The late Mr. Justice Madden's delightful book, *The Diary of Master William Silence*, is suggestive in this matter, as in many others. There is no reason to quarrel with the collaboration of Fletcher in *Henry VIII*; perhaps of Marlowe in *Richard III*; and probably of several dramatists in all three parts of *Henry VI*.

CHAPTER VII

JACOBEAN TO PURITAN

TO turn from Shakespeare to the other dramatists of those spacious days is to find that none beside him quite realized how spacious they were. One cannot see *The Tempest* without feeling that Shakespeare was conscious of a new universe as well as a new hemisphere coming into being. Had he heard of the Copernican theory, which had been confirmed by Kepler and Galileo just two years before? Apparently not. All his cosmic ideas are based on the old Ptolemaic system of the earth hanging in the middle of things and the spangled heaven moving round. At the same time it is difficult to resist a sense that Prospero's farewell to the "elves" and "demi-puppets"—those "weak masters" by whom he had worked the "rough magic" he now abjured—had something to do with the passing of the old science before the new. After all, it had been Mercator's globe which inspired the very naming of the ever-famous theatre, and now . . .!

In those last days at Stratford, watching the flame from the log-fire at New Place, or taking a turn in the garden to "still his beating mind," Shakespeare had very different material for his imagination to work upon in regard to the greater globe, "and all who it inherit," than had the scapegrace boy of thirty odd years before, listening to the dairymaids' tales of Robin Goodfellow. Ariel himself, released from the cloven pine, flashing in the summer sun or flickering at the mast-head, suggests, as Puck never does, an impersonation of forces now harnessed to the service of man. If, on that enchanted island, Shakespeare was projecting his fancy "as far as thought could reach," he was most certainly the only dramatist who was doing anything of the kind. Elsewhere in Europe the drama was, in its most advanced manifestations, centuries behind the times. It was, for the most part, torn between romanticism, then in full flower in the Spanish drama of Lope de Vega and Calderon, which tells of an already obsolete age of chivalry, and classicism, destined to return from its tomb and stalk the French stage for a hundred and fifty years, actually wearing its shroud.

Spanish Drama

As for the stupendously prolific Lope, no English critic can, with life at its present length, pretend to be acquainted with even a reasonable fraction of the 1,500 plays he wrote—not counting the *autos sacramentales*, or miracle-plays, and interludes. This is, of course, consciously. They have reappeared in countless forms. The first act of Bernard Shaw's *Arms and the Man* is almost an exact recapitulation of one of Lope's most famous scenes. On the whole, one can hardly do wrong in accepting George Henry Lewes's happy verdict—

> If you go to him with critical spectacles dogmatically bestriding your nose, you will be ill-contented. If you expect to find a Shakespeare, a Molière or a Schiller, you may save yourself the trouble. But there is an endless charm in Lope—his gaiety. His unflagging animal spirits, playful irony and careless gaiety keep your mind in a constant smile.

It is different with Calderon—soldier and priest as well as dramatist—supreme as an author of the *autos sacramentales*, and hailed as the "Spanish Shakespeare." Calderon undoubtedly touches a higher plane of praise than Lope ever did. Though he was not so prolific, his 112 surviving dramas and 72 *autos* have dignity and fancy. Some of them have been admirably translated by Edward Fitzgerald, of *Omar Khayyám* fame. But I must confess to having experienced a certain disappointment over the most famous of them, *La Vida Es Sueño* (*Life is a Dream*), when I saw it acted upon the stage in one of the late William Poel's productions. In spite of continual harping upon the charming title, I did not see how this concerned the story of Prince Sigismund's discovery in prison—to finish up, after many adventures, as a conqueror—more than in any other romantic dramas of escapes and revelations and abrupt changes.

Though *Don Quixote* remains one of the best bedside books ever written, the Spanish drama of the sixteenth and seventeenth centuries does not give us of to-day on the stage a value

comparable to that of Cervantes in literary fiction. It just
does not represent the kind of romance suitable to our philosophic and introspective northern temperament. But it was
enormously important to its own day. The plots of Lope and
Calderon were pillaged by Beaumont and Fletcher, Middleton,
Webster, and others of our own Jacobeans. These tended to
replace the gallantry and sparkle of their originals with somewhat too lingering an emphasis upon unnatural horrors.

Charles Lamb

But there is one critic, unmatched within his own limits of
self-expression, with whom this very fact was an advantage.
One cannot think of the minor Elizabethans and Jacobeans
without instantly clearing a space for Charles Lamb. He was
a champion who is certainly more sure of immortality than
several of themselves. However much one may disagree with
some of his choices and some of his conclusions, it would be
difficult to calculate how much of the fame of the Mermaid
men is due to Lamb's personal reaction. His salute to them is
irresistible. It is part of Lamb himself. Everything and everyone he writes about are mixed up with the irony of the queer,
punctual, golden-hearted East India clerk, going back after
the "day's dry drudgery at the desk's dead wood" to keep high
festival in groping through dusty folios. What glory to light
upon scenes like that of Calantha, in Ford's *The Broken Heart*,
going on with the dance after hearing of the death of all she
held dear, and then falling dead herself!—

> I do not know where to find, in any play, a catastrophe so
> grand, so solemn, so surprising, as in this. . . . The fortitude
> of the Spartan boy who let a beast gnaw out his bowels till he
> died, without expressing a groan, is a faint bodily image of this
> dilaceration of the spirit, and exenteration of the inmost mind,
> which Calantha, with a holy violence against her nature, keeps
> closely covered till the last duties of a wife and queen are fulfilled.

With this haunting passage in mind, I recall in the later
'nineties seeing a performance of *The Broken Heart* at St.
George's Hall. It was an excellent performance. If I remember
rightly, Eleanor Calhoun, a finely temperamental actress,
was in the part of Calantha. But it did not stir me to anything

like the extent to be expected from Lamb's criticism. So, too, with Webster's *The Duchess of Malfi*. The tribute of Charles Lamb to that gruesome last scene of mental torture, with its dance of madmen, is in itself unforgettable—

> She has lived among horrors until she has become native and endowed unto that element. She speaks the dialect of despair; her tongue has a snatch of Tartarus and the souls in bale.

It has been my lot to see *The Duchess of Malfi* a number of times—both well and badly played. Yet never has that particular scene appeared to me to be other than a piece of gratuitous sadism on Webster's part. We have to recognize that Lamb was not only the solitary companion to a sister afflicted with homicidal mania, but in constant dread of what might happen to his own active and imprisoned mind. Those old horrors of a vanished stage must have had for him a peculiar solace of make-believe.

Ben Jonson

On the other hand, we must all admit that there are a number of Elizabethan and Jacobean plays, besides Shakespeare's, which need no abnormal excuse for acceptance. They treasured up values which have not lost their appeal even now. They had in them the seeds of future harvests to be reaped long after. In Jonson's "learned sock"—for all the dullness of his tragedies—realistic comedy was born. Ulrici, the German critic and philosopher, has some candid things to say about Jonson—

> Where he combats folly, vice and senselessness, he forgets his learning, he warms up, his anger gives him concise, sententious language, a certain heavy grandeur. Everything—diction and characterization, drawing and colouring, light and shade— is not only correct and appropriate, but full of life and energy. His element is reality.
>
> Of a different, higher poetical truth—a truth in the form of beauty—he is unconscious. What is the same thing, when he wishes to represent it (as in his Masques), it becomes in his hands an abstract allegory. He cannot collect either ideal or human generalities into an organic whole.

With all his limitations, there is a strong, virile, highly critical intelligence about "rare Ben," together with that overwhelming wealth of human as well as classical knowledge, which makes one feel almost guilty about not caring for *Every Man in His Humour, Volpone, The Alchemist,* and *Epicœne.* It is always the same story. At each Jonson revival, one realizes that here is a grand old master to whom one ought to pay homage. But he never gets near one's inner heart, as Shakespeare does. It is like walking through a store where choice goods are piled lavishly on every side, duly labelled. They are all very wonderful; but they are not always the things that we happen to want. Some of us feel differently, perhaps. *Volpone,* both in adaptations and otherwise, has had recent adventures before a certain public; but not to very great or very pleasant purpose.

I myself much prefer the breeze and vividness of *Bartholomew Fair,* with its close-up, Hogarthian panorama of the vigorous, multi-coloured life of the London streets and markets. One feels that all the time Jonson needed something seen, which he could convey and criticize. He had not enough of the woman in him for creation. He tried his hand at everything. His lyrics have a fine-cut grace and there was nothing he did weakly; but his pastoral fragment, *The Sad Shepherd,* must yield place to Fletcher's exquisite *The Faithful Shepherdess,* which seems more charming every time it is revived. Dekker, too, was a formidable challenger both as a lyrist and, in *The Shoemaker's Holiday,* as a faithful picturer of London life. On the romantic plane, remembering *The Knight of the Burning Pestle,* Beaumont and Fletcher had quite understandably a more popular quality.

One thing heralded by the later Elizabethans and Jacobeans was the domestic drama. This afforded, with the London comedies of Jonson and Dekker, a home-bred alternative to adapted Italian romance and the cloak-and-sword butcheries from Spain. Thomas Heywood's *A Woman Killed with Kindness,* Massinger's *The City Madam* and *A New Way to Pay Old Debts* set observed and native types working out the impact of incident upon character in the contemporary homes of English country-gentlemen and merchants. It has been said that the drama had faded away already by the time the Puritans put a stop to it altogether. But this is not quite so. In Massinger, as

Arthur Symons very well suggested, the Jonsonian comedy of humours was merging into the comedy of manners. It is possible that, if the times had been less distracted, Massinger and others, including Shirley, who survived only to die in the Fire of London, might have bridged over what was to prove a disastrous gap.

Court Masques

There remain the Court masques—those gorgeous extravagances which were the parents of modern opera and ballet. They helped to support Jonson in his later years and to stimulate spectacular production with the arrival of Inigo Jones. But they were all too often affairs of diplomacy to an extent which put them outside criticism. This may be gathered from one of the liveliest first-hand accounts that survive of any performance given during the period between Shakespeare and the Commonwealth. It is by Busino, the Italian, who was present on the first night of *Pleasure Reconciled to Virtue*, written by Ben Jonson, staged by Inigo Jones, and presented at Court before King James and Count Gondomar, the Spanish Ambassador. The future King Charles I, who was at that time supposed to be going to marry the Infanta, was Chief Masquer—

> They had some mummeries performed in the first act. For instance a very chubby Bacchus appeared on a car drawn by four gownsmen who sang in an undertone before His Majesty, and there was another on foot also in good case and dressed in red, in short clothes, who made a speech reeling about like a drunkard, tankard in hand, so that he resembled the said Bacchus's cup-bearer, and this first scene was very gay and burlesque. Next followed twelve extravagant masquers, one of whom was in a barrel all but his extremities, his companions being in like manner cased in huge wicker flasks, very well made, and they danced awhile to the sound of the cornets. This being at an end, each took his lady, the Prince pairing with the principal one among those who stood in a row. . . .
>
> Being well nigh tired they began to lag, whereupon the King, who is naturally choleric, got impatient and shouted aloud: "Why don't they dance? What did you make me come here for? Devil take you all, dance!" Upon this the Marquis of Buckingham, His Majesty's most favoured minion, immediately sprang forward, cutting a score of very lofty and minute capers, with so much grace and agility that he not only appeased the ire of his angry

Lord, but moreover rendered himself the admiration and delight of everybody. . . . The story ended at half past two in the morning, and half disgusted and weary we turned home.

This masque had cost £4,000—at least £24,000 of our money —but Ben Jonson's share in it did not redound to his credit. Nathaniel Brent wrote to his friend Carleton that "of Ben Jonson divers thinke fit he returne to his ould trade of brickelaying againe." If this was the kind of thing that was happening, no wonder Shakespeare, who had died two years before, retired when he did!

"Comus"

With all its incidents of extravagance and vulgarity, and its deplorable record of subservience to political ends, the masque as a form of art had its distinct and abiding dramatic value. Shakespeare used it in his first play and in his last, and it undoubtedly influenced the technique of *Macbeth*. The appearance of Henrietta Maria and the Court ladies in masque, long before the Commonwealth, heralded the introduction of actresses on our popular stage at the Restoration.

Not least, it was the masque of *Comus* that showed, even more surely than the *Samson Agonistes* of his later years, what the theatre lost through Milton failing to fulfil his first ambition of becoming a prolific dramatist. Strangely enough, Comus actually appeared as a character in that very masque of Ben Jonson's which Busino describes. But he is there an entirely different conception—just a god of gluttony and drink, brought into the chorus—

Room, room! Make room for the Bouncing Belly.
First father of sauce and deviser of jelly.

Probably *Comus* is more happily familiar to us of this generation than it has been to any since it was originally performed at Ludlow Castle in 1634, when the Earl of Bridgewater, President of Wales, and his Countess and family took part. Some of us saw this firstling of Milton's dramatic invention produced within memory at Ludlow Castle itself. Many have seen it presented with far greater beauty and effectiveness in the Open Air Theatre at Regents Park. There it proved, next to Shakespeare's *A Midsummer Night's Dream*, the most consistently popular success among Mr. Sydney W. Carroll's memorable enterprises.

Comus is, of course, much more than a masque. Among other things, in its frank and noble championship of chastity, it stands out as a great pioneer expression. No dramatist young or old has suggested anything to compare with Milton's exquisite *envoi*—

> Mortals that would follow me
> Love virtue, she alone is free.
> She can teach ye how to climb
> Higher than the sphery chime;
> Or, if virtue feeble were,
> Heaven itself would stoop to her.

"Samson Agonistes"

A lifetime of arduous labour and civic strife was to stretch between *Comus* and *Samson Agonistes*. This also many of us have seen played in ideal circumstances—beneath the great Norman arch of Tewkesbury, and, a more recent performance, at St. Martin-in-the-Fields, with Abraham Sofaer in the title-part. As an attempted reversion to the forms and unities of the Greek drama it has its self-imposed limitations. One can understand that Milton never expected it to be put upon the stage in his time. It was utterly against the baroque fashions of the heroic drama of the Restoration—not to mention the later Elizabethan orgies of horror and debasement. Milton himself, in his foreword, saw fit to—

> vindicate Tragedy from the small esteem, or rather infamy, which in the account of many it undergoes at this day, with other common interludes; happening through the poet's error of intermixing comic stuff with tragic sadness and gravity, or introducing trivial and vulgar persons; which by all judicious hath been counted absurd, and brought in without discretion, corruptly to gratify the people.

On the other hand I do not believe that *Samson Agonistes* was written without the thought of presentation in the author's mind. At any rate the blind Milton would hardly have imagined his lines in print, as some modern poets confess to doing. His fancy would have heard them spoken in a theatre of his own, something upon the Greek model. I always feel that

Samson Agonistes has a practical dramatic importance which has not even yet been fully recognized. Here is Milton expressing his own life-story through a dramatic medium. From a wholly modern point of view it has masterly touches, not least in the character and description of Delilah—or Dalila, as Milton calls her. With a little shortening of "wave-length," of which he was fully capable, how much our theatre might have been enriched if Milton had been given a chance of fulfilling his first idea of creating a high and pure tradition of drama as a fruit of the Puritan mind !

Milton's Hope

Milton himself, we know, made out a list of ninety-three subjects for tragedies—sixty from the Bible, of which Samson was one, and thirty-three from British history. We know that he had planned *Paradise Lost* as a play. To the theatre he wished to give, as he put it—

> a work not to be raised from the heat of youth, or the vapours of wine, like that which flows at waste from the pen of some vulgar amorist or the trencher-fury of a riming parasite, nor to be obtained by the invocation of Dame Memory and her Siren daughters, but by devout prayer to that Eternal Spirit, who can enrich with all utterance and knowledge, and sends out his Seraphim with the hallowed fire of his altar to touch and purify the lips of whom he pleases.

It is all very well to say that this kind of thing does not belong to the theatre. Why should it not? The theatre was popular enough when it was officially a Temple of Venus. No one objected to it then on the score of its being religious. Why should it not be regarded, under Christian auspices, as a Temple of the Holy Ghost? This is a very vital question for any who wish to take dramatic criticism seriously.

So far as Milton is concerned, it is quite evident that he himself had far more dramatic capabilities in him than he ever allowed to emerge as things were. They express themselves, in a kind of frustrated way, by the astonishing violence of style that came upon him in some of his pamphlets. He knew what it was to "leave a calm and pleasing solitariness, fed with cheerful and confident thoughts, to embark in a troubled sea of noises and hoarse disputes." An intense humanity must have lain behind those three marriages—his disillusionment over Mary Powell, the Royalist "bright young person," the brief happiness with Catherine Woodcock, his "late espoused saint," and the consolation afforded to his last years by Elizabeth Minshull, the wife he never saw. How far from truth must be the notion, still prevailing in many quarters, that because Milton was a Puritan he was therefore passionless!

"Histrio-mastix"

It is well to remember that two years before the performance of *Comus*—that is to say, in 1632—William Prynne's *Histrio-mastix, The Scourge for Actors*, had been given to the world. It represented the less enlightened and, unfortunately, more effectual attitude of Puritanism at large to the theatre. This bulky and ill-digested mass of collected vituperation had nothing like the liveliness of Gosson's *Schoole of Abuse* of forty-three years before, or of Jeremy Collier's *Short View of the Immorality and Profaneness of the English Stage*, which was to come sixty-six years after. I have found it inexpressibly wearisome. Prynne was put in the pillory and had his ears cut off because his reference to "women actors" was held to be a reference to Queen Henrietta Maria's performances in a Court masque the same year. To my thinking, he deserved the treatment equally for having turned out a book so sour and unhelpful and merely destructive.

He seems to have been at any rate a man of immense practical ability, aggressive, and determined. A remarkable thing is that in spite of having had his ears twice mutilated and having suffered every sort of obloquy, he became Recorder and Member of Parliament for Bath, was ultimately appointed Keeper of the Tower Records, and died a hale old fellow in his seventieth year. But *Histrio-mastix* is dreary stuff, with its pronouncements against the stage of "55 Synodes and Councils, 71 Fathers and Christian Writers, 150 Foraigne and Domestique Protestant and Popish Authors and 40 Heathen Philosophers, Historians and Poets." These, he claims, combined to assert that—

Stage-playes (the very Pompes of the Devill, which we renounced in Baptisme, if we believe the Fathers) are sinful, heathenish, lewde, ungodly Spectacles, and most pernicious Corruptions, condemned in all ages as intolerable mischiefes to Churches, to Republics, to the Manners, Minds and Souls of Men, and that the professions of Play-poets and Stage-players are unlawful, infamous and misbeseeming Christians.

At the same time he attests with remarkable precision the hold upon the contemporary public of these inventions of "idolatrous and voluptuous Pagans, impregnated with their infernal issue from Hell itself"—

> How many there are who according to their several qualities, spend 2d., 4d., 6d., 12d., 18d., 2s., or sometimes 4s., or 5s., at a Playhouse, day by day, if Coach-hire, Boat-hire, Tobacco, Wine, Beere, and such like expenses which plays do usually occasion, be cast into the reckoning, and who can never honestly get by their lawful callings half so much!

The "Pagan" Theatre

At almost every point Prynne, at a time which was just as sophisticated upon many of these matters as our own, takes up the old attitude of the Fathers that the theatre was still "pagan," and therefore necessarily an anti-Christian institution. This, as I have already noted, may very probably have influenced Milton, himself none the less strongly attracted by the "well-trod stage," and was to be repeated later on by Jeremy Collier. It is still, beyond all manner of doubt, responsible for a large amount of antagonism to the theatre on the part of many members of all churches. Even now, Roman Catholic priests are not, by canon-law, permitted to attend a public performance in a theatre, though they may in a cinema. Similar considerations may or may not have induced a recent decision on the part of the Church of England Assembly. The attitude of the Free Churches remains in a large measure definitely hostile to the theatre. This is a matter in which honest and sincere and broadminded criticism can, to my thinking, yet prove of very great value.

The simple and obvious truth is that historically the theatre as a whole *is* a pagan institution. So far as there is continuity, that continuity goes right back, as we have seen, to the Roman theatre, and to the jesters and minstrels who represented the wandering inheritors of such scraps of popular tradition as were left. The liturgy-born miracle-play was only a contributory stream which happened to arrive before the recurrence of the classic repertory and its modern developments with the Renaissance. It was by no means the real or main source of modern drama.

Humanity

On the other hand we must take for granted that the pagan deities, as deities, are, presumably, dead. To be afraid of them is to believe in them. The idea to which St. Augustine subscribed, and upon which Prynne harps, was that they still exist as projections of the spiritual power of the Devil. This is hardly likely to disturb many modern playgoers. We have come to recognize that what was good in the classical and pagan drama represented simple human reactions, imaginings, passions—the sense of beauty in nature and of duty in conduct, the charm of music and of dance, the joy of laughter, the consolation of human sympathy, the criticism of life, of history and of science, the expression of the individual human heart in physical communion.

These things may have been once looked upon as worship of whatever gods might be in the Egyptian, Greek or Roman pantheon. They are still the material of much of our modern dramatic entertainment. The average musical comedy or beauty-chorus revue still promulgates what used to be regarded as the worship of Venus—it would be ridiculous to pretend otherwise. The average war-melodrama is exactly what would once have been recognized, and is still by cartoonists, as an act of worship to Mars. We are now content to believe that there is no Venus and no Mars, that they just represent human instincts coming within the purview of representatively human drama. Any antagonism to the stage on their account is an antagonism not to Venus and Mars but to something human, bad or good, sincere or insincere, as the case may be.

It does not mean that a theatrical performance of either of these types is necessarily a call to unbridled licence or savagery. In a Christian country they must naturally accord themselves with Christian morality in so far as that prevails.

In this way the support of the theatre by the Christian churches is all to the benefit both of them and of the theatre. The churches could never absorb in themselves all that happens— and should happen—in a theatre, which is not a church any more than it is now an exclusively pagan temple.

"Apology for Actors"

Even in the England of those seventeenth-century days, before the closure of the playhouses, the spirit of the theatre itself was by no means essentially anti-moral. It was James Shirley, the Royalist playwright, who gave to immortality those noble lines—

> Only the actions of the just
> Smell sweet and blossom in the dust.

No happier view even of the gayest type of comedy could well be set down than that of Thomas Heywood, author of 220 plays, who neither did nor wrote anything of which he needed to be deeply ashamed. This is what he said in his *Apology for Actors* (1612)—

What is, then, the subject of this harmless mirth? Either in the shape of a clown to show others their slovenly and unhandsome behaviour, that they may reform that simplicity in themselves which others make their sport; else it entreats of love, deriding foolish inamorates, who spend their ages, their spirits, nay, themselves, in the servile and ridiculous employments of their mistresses. And these are mingled with sportful accidents, to recreate such as of themselves are wholly devoted to melancholy, which corrupts the blood, or to refresh such weary spirits as are tired with labour or study, to moderate the cares and heaviness of the mind, that they may return to their trades and faculties with more zeal and earnestness after some small, soft and pleasant retirement.

Sometimes they discourse of pantaloons, usurers that have unthrifty sons, which both the fathers and the sons may behold to their instructions: sometimes of courtezans, to divulge their subtleties and snares in which young men may be entangled, showing them the means to avoid them. If we present a pastoral, we show the harmless love of shepherds diversely moralized, distinguishing between the craft of the city and the innocency of the sheepcote. Briefly, there is neither tragedy, history, comedy, moral or pastoral, from which an infinite use cannot be gathered.

I speak not in defence of any lascivious shows, scurrilous jests or scandalous invectives. If there be any such, I banish them quite from my patronage.

Coryat's "Crudities"

Suppose, for another pleasant glimpse, we go farther afield and take our stand in Venice with old Coryat, the Somerset farmer who became jester at Prince Henry's Court at St. James's, and proved so genial a critic of drama as well as of manners in the record of his tour of Europe, with the visit to India and the Great Mogul to follow. In Coryat's book of *Crudities* (1611) we see the "charlatans" or "mountebanks" of the *Commedia dell' Arte* still engaged as cheapjacks in putting up their impromptu plays to lure purchasers for the wares of Autolycus in the open market-place—

> When I was in Venice they oftentimes ministered infinite pleasures unto me. . . . After the whole rabble of them is gotten up to the stage, whereof some wear vizards, being disguised like fools in a play, some that are women (for there are divers also among them) are attired with habits according to that person that they sustaine; after, I say, that they are all upon the stage, the music begins. Sometimes vocal, sometimes instrumental, and sometimes both together. This music is a preamble and introduction to the ensuing matter. . . . These merry fellows do most commonly continue two good hours upon the stage, and at last, when they have fed the audience with such passing variety of sport that they are even cloyed with the superfluity of their conceits, and have sold as much ware as they can, they remove their trinkets and stage till the next meeting.

The "merry fellows" of whom Coryat speaks were not, of course, anything new to some among his London readers. Martinelli, the famous harlequin, had already appeared in London with his troupe by special permission of the Lord Mayor over thirty years before. They were not then much admired by the London crowd. The presence of women on the stage did not please, especially as Nash tells us that they "did forbear no immodest speech or unchaste action that may procure laughter." The idealization of the *Commedia* was a long way off as yet, though Paris was to give it a memorable, prolonged, and fruitful welcome.

Oberammergau

One product of the seventeenth century must not be forgotten, especially in view of what I have said about specifically religious drama. It was in 1634, after their miraculous preservation from the Black Death, that the peasants of Oberammergau, in the Bavarian Alps, made their vow to present a play of Christ's Passion once every ten years. The vow has been kept ever since, with only occasional variations due to war, like that which summoned the Christus of 1870 to come down from the Cross to serve in the Bavarian artillery. Many things may happen before each decade brings normally the next presentation. From being a simple village folk-drama, the Oberammergau Passion Play has grown into a world festival, with strange results, some of them, ironically, financial. Not only are external conditions changing with the growth of audiences, the consequent worldly temptations and the film's persistent approaches. The play itself, the music, and the production have all been altered from time to time. It will be worth while to see in the future—if nothing happens to prevent the Passion Play altogether, as did the later world-war during its progress—what further changes of spirit will occur in the observed and the observers.

CHAPTER VIII

THE AGE OF ARTIFICE

WE now reach the so-called "age of criticism"—that is to say, the age when the cultivated world, having discovered that a new great force in art had come into being, set itself to discuss the why and how. It did so with such furious eagerness as almost to stifle the modern drama at birth. It was an age when everybody was a critic. The authors themselves wasted a ridiculous amount of their time and energy on debating critical theory in "defences" and "*examens*," prefaces and dedications, prologues and epilogues. Whole shelf-loads of pamphlets fostered the interminable discussion of those supposed laws—the unities of time, place, and action.

This was only natural, of course. It was the disease being mistaken for the doctor. True and enlightened criticism is the enemy of laws—nearly all of which are, as I have said, obvious where they are not compulsory, and, if they are laws, will assert themselves anyhow. The usefulness of good criticism is that it replaces laws by helpful understanding. It corresponds in a measure to equity in the judicial world. But unfortunately there have always been more dull and uncreative people than there have been men of genius. The dull and uncreative people naturally take to law-making, as satisfying their capabilities and vanity at the same time. So these eternal controversies go on reverberating.

Realism

Underneath them, none the less, living purposes reveal themselves. It is so even with these unities. Though they were based on an entire misconception of Aristotle, supplemented by Horace's comparatively irresponsible lines in his *Ars Poetica*, the essence of it all was that the stage was still trying to put before itself a corresponding aim. Even in verse-plays on a platform-stage the idea survived, of creating an illusion by scenic realism, or, to use a longer word, "verisimilitude."

This purpose of "holding the mirror up to nature," which Hamlet was content to impose only upon the actor, would be naturally disturbed by change of place, time, or story on a platform-stage in a yard or hall, supposing an audience dependent upon sight for information.

But audiences are not dependent upon sight, as broadcast drama sufficiently proves. A hint is all they should need. For myself I find the author who cannot give all necessary hints in these matters, the actor who cannot convey them, and the audience who cannot take them hardly worth critical consideration. Corneille in his *Examen* upon *Le Cid* explains his own difficulties in speeding up action to get it into even a semblance of twenty-four hours, and in bringing Ferdinand to Seville. Shakespeare was extremely clever in his use of "double time"—pointing forward to a short interval before a change of scene, and backwards to a long one after it. But these are trivial dodges and tricks of theatre-craft, for which the practised hand arranges without thinking. They are problems for producers and apprentice-dramatists. For the critic, who has mostly to deal with spiritual values, to worry too much about these minor technicalities is to superimpose a photographer's study upon a mountain-view. Granted imagination, the mind of the intelligent spectator is surveying not only what is supposed to happen during the course of the action but— from *Oedipus* to *Back to Methuselah*—ages before and after.

Richelieu

One especial debt we owe to the controversies over the unities, over the use of rhyme, and over the introduction of comic scenes into tragedy. They provided John Dryden, who was always entertaining as a critic, if not always as a dramatist, with topics for his famous *Essay of Dramatick Poesy* (1668), and for the *Defence* of that essay, and other lively prose-pieces. The real task-masters of the unities were, of course, Cardinal Richelieu and his Academy, founded in 1635, who hauled even Corneille over the coals. Dryden is content to mix them all up together—

> The Muses, who ever follow peace, went to plant in another country. It was then that the great Cardinal Richelieu began to

take them into his protection; and that by his encouragement Corneille and some other Frenchmen reformed their theatre, which before was as much below ours as it now surpasses it and the rest of Europe. In the unity of time you find the French so scrupulous that it yet remains a dispute among their poets, whether the artificial day of twelve hours, more or less, be meant by Aristotle, rather than the natural one of twenty-four; and consequently whether all plays ought not to be reduced into that compass. In the unity of place they are fully as scrupulous, for many of their critics limit it to that very spot of ground where the play is supposed to begin. None of them exceed the compass of the same town or city. The unity of action in all their plays is yet more conspicuous; for they do not burden them with underplots as the English do . . . confounding the audience.

This last point is soon countered by Dryden in suggesting lack of variety—

Look upon Corneille's *Cinna* and *Pompey*, they are not so properly to be called plays, as long discourses of reason of state; and *Polyeucte* in matters of religion is as solemn as the long stops upon our organs. Since that time it is grown into a custom, and their actors speak by the hour-glass, like our parsons; nay, they account it the grace of their parts, and think themselves disparaged by the poet if they may not twice or thrice in a play entertain the audience with a speech of an hundred lines. I deny not but this may suit well with the French; for as we, who are a more sullen people, come to be diverted at our plays, so they, who are of an airy and gay temper, come thither to make themselves more serious.

Plot and Purpose

All this argumentative stool-ball occurs, it may be noted, in a classic of English dramatic criticism which takes practically no account of the things that Corneille really stood for. The qualities which made the social world of its time delight in *Le Cid* had nothing to do with the question of whether or no it broke the unities, or how far it shocked Richelieu by the duel which wrung the heart of Chimène, its sore-tried heroine. Its ideals of honour, sacrifice, and disinterested love, expressed in noble and impassioned verse—these were the things which gave it a personal appeal over and above the freshly romantic intrigue of Castro's Spanish original.

As for the long-exploded fallacy of an underplot "confounding the audience," one has to go no farther than Shakespeare's own *The Merchant of Venice* to find a play in which three entirely different stories, taken from three entirely different sources, are woven together in such a way that instead of "confounding" anybody they are mutually helpful. The pound-of-flesh story came from *Il Pecorone*, the caskets story from *Gesta Romanorum*, and the elopement of the Jew's daughter from the *Tales* of Massuccio di Salerno. Yet, as has been pertinently suggested by Mr. H. L. Withers in his edition of the play—

> If Antonio had not signed the bond, Bassanio could not have gone a-wooing, if Bassanio had not won Portia, there would have been no-one to save Antonio, and if Lorenza and Jessica had not wandered to Belmont, Portia could not so readily have quitted Belmont for Venice.

While Corneille submitted to the restraint of the unities with difficulty, the thirty-years-younger Racine seems to have taken to them much more by temperament. His scrupulous style and intense concentration upon the psychology of a few closely-studied characters—especially strong-willed and passionate women, like Hermione in *Andromaque* and the Phèdre in whom Rachel and Bernhardt revelled—were helped rather than otherwise by enforced limits. These were to them like tramlines.

Molière

At times one is heartily glad that Aristotle himself did not lay down any laws for comedy, and Horace's suggestions, such as the keeping of unpleasant incidents off-stage, are more or less adjustable matters of taste and common sense. Perhaps this is one reason why Corneille and Racine were both happy in comedy. Corneille's *Le Menteur* and Racine's *Les Plaideurs* are still deservedly popular. As for Molière, how useful it was for him that, though he had his troubles with the same *unco guid* whose entrenched hypocrisy made him wait five years before he could produce *Tartuffe* in public, he was not bound to confine himself to what Terence and Plautus had done beforehand! He could pillage the Italian *Commedia* for his Sganarelles and Scapins; he could pillory the blue-stockings and quacks and money-grubbers and social climbers of the real world around him, and lighten the agonizing story of his own life with the laughter and wisdom of *Le Misanthrope* and *Le Malade Imaginaire.*

It is possible that the story of his own unhappy marriage, and the irony of his last appearance in the play he wrote in self-mockery have tended to soften the tone of his humour for us more than they should. The result is that when he is acted in the right and traditional fashion upon the stage he tends to seem hard and callous. In *Le Misanthrope,* for instance, we expect a suggestion of a lump in the throat over Alceste and Célimène, and we get just high-voiced raillery. Such is, of course, the right way—the true Molière, as King Louis saw his favourite comedian on the stage. Professor Saintsbury emphasizes this—

> May it be permitted to doubt whether Molière really intended to excite all the admiring sympathy which has been bestowed upon Alceste? Without that sympathy he remains an admirably comic figure; but he becomes hardly more of a tragic one than Malvolio, for whom also some respectable persons have tried to excite it. . . . He is a "man of honour," no doubt; but he is also, if one may dare to say so, a "fool of honour," and not a very amiable one.

Congreve

Something of the same heartlessness is what makes our own Restoration comedy so difficult to accept and present in its true value to a modern audience. We tend to worry as to whether we should sympathize with the "filthy fellows" and flaunting wantons of Wycherley and Congreve, though Valentine in *Love for Love* has a certain claim. So far as Wycherley's besmeared coarsening of Molière's perfectly clean creations is concerned, disgust may well prevent any further reaction in a decent modern mind. Congreve is different. He had equally to write for a foul-living and dirty-minded audience; but his mind was not itself a cess-pool. Again and again he brings in touches of pure wit and bright imagery as well as that grace and rhythm of sparkling speech which condone so much. But the heartlessness is still there, above all in the women. According to George Meredith it is not heartlessness but just common sense—

> Comedy is the fountain of sound sense; not the less perfectly sound on account of the sparkle; and comedy lifts women to a station offering them free play for their wit. . . . Millamant in *The Way of the World* is an admirable, almost a lovable heroine—"with her fan spread and her streamers out."

Strange that two such differing dramatists as Congreve and Milton should coincide so nearly in their metaphor for an apparently eternal type of womanhood! Here is Milton's description of Dalila, believed by many to be an orientalized portrait, painted from embittered memory, of Mary Powell, his first wife. It was published just upon thirty years before Congreve's play—

> But who is this? What thing of sea or land—
> Female of sex it seems—
> That so bedecked, ornate and gay,
> Comes this way sailing,
> Like a stately ship
> Of Tarsus, bound for the isles
> Of Javan or Gadire,
> With all her bravery on, and tackle trim,
> Sails filled and streamers waving,
> Courted by all the winds that hold them play;
> An amber scent of odorous perfume
> Her harbinger . . .?

Collier's "Short View"

So far as criticism is concerned, vivacious argument was kept up by Dryden, Thomas Rymer, and others upon such long-debated questions as the presence of comic scenes in tragedy and of rhyme in heroic verse. But the thing which stirred the whole world of the theatre to its depths was Jeremy Collier's *Short View of the Profaneness and Immorality of the English Stage*. It was published in 1698, just two years before the production of *The Way of the World* and nine years after the accession of William III, to whom Jeremy refused, as a non-juror, to pay homage. There is all the difference between Prynne's gloating pedantries and this admirable and well-reasoned attack on tendencies deserving of everything that was said about them.

Here, for instance, is a criticism which goes much deeper than a mere list of nasty phrases—

> To put lewdness into a thriving condition, to give it an equipage of quality, and to treat it with ceremony and respect, is the way to confound the understanding, to fortify the charm and to make the mischief invincible.

Against old Jeremy's searching championship of good taste, combined, as it was, with a genuine respect for clean and reputable art, Congreve's unwise and feeble reply was the failure it could not help being. So, with the brilliance of Farquhar and the coarseness of Vanbrugh, the comedy of manners disappeared in a much-needed wash-tub—to emerge a whole generation after in Sheridan's purged and perfected aftermath. After a little more than a decade, in 1711, Steele in *The Spectator* was following up, with somewhat belated boldness, what had already become a minority fashion. He chose for his objective Sir George Etheredge, who had been dead for seventeen years, and his thirty-five-year-old play, *The Man of Mode*. This is what Steele then said—

> I will take for granted that a fine gentleman should be honest in his actions, and refined in his language. Instead of this, our hero is a direct knave in his designs and a clown in his language.

Critics and Actors

An important development of criticism—at any rate English criticism—through the middle years of the eighteenth century was the transfer of main attention from plays to actors. No great new dramatist was to make his arrival until Goldsmith, with the coming of *She Stoops to Conquer*, in 1773. The dreary intervening trough of tame tragedy, Italianate farce, and the sentimental comedy to which Steele himself harmlessly contributed has come to represent so much "museum stuff." Excellent for an academic thesis or documentary appendix, it is otherwise just dead and never likely to live again.

With the passing of Betterton, and the homage paid him, we are made to realize that, unlike the play, the actor can be given a further life in criticism. Indeed, it is remarkable how often it is only after he is dead that critics discover how great an actor was, or seemed to be. It may be that this is just largely part of the magic of memory, which has a power of casting off the material rubble and finding the soul of the performance. This is not by any means necessarily the soul of the actor himself. It is a spiritual creation, born partly of the play, partly of the actor and all that appertains to him upon the stage, and partly of the audience, which the critic—or whoever is the recorder of the impressions—represents in so far as he is a sympathetic member of it.

The achievement was, and is, communal; but the credit went, and still goes, to the actor. He is the obvious focus. After he is dead and cannot benefit, the idealizing process is immune from contradiction.

Betterton

So we find with Betterton. In Steele's famous essay in *The Tatler*, there is no comparison of him with other actors. It does not tell us how Betterton avoided being acted off the stage by Iago, which so often happens in a modern production. It simply records the different effect of seeing Othello played by a "wonderful" actor—even in a garbled version—

> The wonderful agony which he appeared in when he examined the circumstances of the handkerchief in *Othello*; the mixture of love that intruded upon his mind, upon the innocent answers Desdemona makes, betrayed in his gesture such a variety and vicissitude of passions, as would admonish a man to be afraid of his own heart.

As will be seen, the word "wonderful"—for which we nowadays condemn our gallery enthusiasts—is the only part of this criticism that really belongs to Betterton, apart from Shakespeare as a dramatist and Steele as a sensitive playgoer. For a far better suggestion of Betterton himself we can go to his fellow-actor, Colley Cibber. It is clear from Cibber's *Apology* that the magic of Betterton lay chiefly in his dignified sincerity of voice and manner—

> Betterton had a voice which gave more spirit to terror than to the softer passions. . . . In Othello he excelled himself; which you will easily believe when you consider that, in spite of his

complexion, Othello has more natural beauties than the best actor can find in all the magazine of poetry. . . . There arose from the harmony of the whole a commanding mien of majesty, which the fairer-faced or (as Shakespeare calls 'em) the "curled darlings" of his time ever wanted as something to be equally masters of.

Addison on Critics

With the arrival of journalism as a profession, dramatic criticism should have been born; but it hardly was. Between the gossip-paragraphs, generally spiteful, as some are to-day, where the flesh-and-blood stage is concerned, and graceful essays, "discovering" the theatre as a place of fashionable resort, little criticism worth preserving appeared till well on in the eighteenth century. "Critics," even as late as Garrick's time, meant coffee-house gossips. Even those who got into print at any length did not always do honour to their calling. In *The Spectator* in 1714, Addison, whose *Cato* had been a political success the year before, administers a reproof to the critics of his own day. It has a certain appropriateness to our own time as well, and perhaps to all times—

> I do not, indeed, wonder that the actors should be professed enemies to those among our nation who are commonly known by the name of critics since it is the rule among these gentlemen to fall upon a play, not because it is ill-written, but because it takes. Several of them lay it down as a maxim, that whatever dramatic performance has a long run, must of necessity be good for nothing; as though the first precept in poetry were *not to please*. . . . It is our misfortune, that some who set up for professed critics among us are so stupid, that they do not know how to put ten words together with elegance or common propriety, and withal so illiterate, that they have no taste of the learned languages, and therefore criticize upon old authors only at second-hand. They judge of them by what others have written, and not by any notions they have of the authors themselves. The words *unity*, *action*, *sentiment*, and *diction*, pronounced with an air of authority, give them a figure among unlearned readers, who are apt to believe they are very deep because they are unintelligible.
>
> The ancient critics are full of the praises of their contemporaries; they discovered beauties which escaped the observation of the vulgar, and very often find out reasons for palliating or excusing such little slips and oversights as were committed in the writings of eminent authors. On the contrary, most of the smatterers

in criticism who appear among us, make it their business to vilify and depreciate every new production that gains applause, to descry imaginary blemishes, and to prove by far-fetched arguments that what pass for beauties in any celebrated piece are faults and errors.

Macklin and Critics

In spite of all this—and Addison had probably every reason for his outburst at a time when the spirit of the satire and the lampoon was everywhere dominant—true and helpful criticism was on its way. The coming out of Rowe's edition of Shakespeare in 1709 had in the end its effect in giving at any rate a challenge to such travesties as Lord Lansdowne's *Jew of Venice*, with its comic Shylock. It is pleasant to know that when Charles Macklin determined in 1741 to restore *The Merchant of Venice* to the stage, with "the Jew that Shakespeare drew," critics of a kind did join in the welcome. He himself told his biographer, Cooke—

> On my return to the green-room after the play was over, it was crowded with nobility and critics, who all complimented me in the warmest and most unbounded manner, and the situation I found myself in, I must confess was one of the most flattering and intoxicating of my whole life. No money, no title, could purchase what I felt. And let no man tell me after this what Fame will not inspire a man to do, and how far the attainment of it will not remunerate his greatest labours. By G-d, sir, though I was not worth £50 in the world at that time, yet, let me tell you, I was Charles the Great for that night.

It is a pity that we have no classic criticism of that eventful evening, with its triumph of sincerity and truth in acting and loyalty to Shakespeare. The cast would have repaid critical study. We do not know what Quin did with Antonio, whether he sawed the air and recited the lines in his impassive tragic manner or admitted some of those natural touches which made him so good a Falstaff. We know that Kitty Clive, that "merry little devil," was accustomed to give imitations of well-known lawyers of the day as Portia in Lord Lansdowne's version. Whether Macklin—or Fleetwood, the manager— allowed her to do so on this occasion must remain in doubt.

Garrick

We know more of the arrival of Macklin's brilliant young disciple, Garrick, at Goodman's Fields only a few months after. From the first Garrick was his own excellent Press agent. On the very next morning *The Daily Post* came out with a statement that the tragedy of *King Richard III* was performed gratis at the late theatre in Goodman's Fields, that the character of Richard was taken by a gentleman who never appeared before, and that the reception was "the most extraordinary and great that was ever known on such an occasion." A few days later *The Champion* went into further particulars—

> His voice is neither whining, bellowing, nor grumbling, but perfectly easy in its transitions, natural in its cadence and beautiful in its elocution. He is not less happy in his mien and gait, in which he is neither strutting nor mincing, neither still nor slouching. When three or four are on the stage with him, he is attentive to whatever is spoke, and never drops his characters when he has finished his speech by either looking contemptuously on an inferior performer, unnecessarily spitting, or suffering his eyes to wander through the whole circle of spectators. His action is never superfluous, awkward or too frequently repeated, but graceful, decent and becoming.

Here was, at least, a piece of honest criticism. If it does not convey to us the greatness of Garrick, it gives an enlightening view of the manners of his contemporaries upon the stage. But this sort of thing is not creative. It is not the kind of dramatic criticism that lives on its own account. Apart from the enormous mass of stories and phrases about Garrick—not forgetting the "puffs" that he wrote himself—the best record of his emotional work and its method and appeal is undoubtedly that of the German, Lichtenberg. Garrick could be "terrific," but so have been many other actors. There was clearly no end to his cleverness in bustling comedy, and in characters as difficult and different as Sir John Brute and Abel Drugger. His powers of sheer mimicry, however varied, were shared by Estcourt and others both before and after his own time, and in ours. His real hold upon hearts as well as minds was undoubtedly that "on the stage he was natural, simple, affecting."

His power of moving an audience by actual tears—above all

at a time when to be "manly" was a matter of vital importance
—deserves more attention than has yet been paid to it. Here
is Lichtenberg's remembrance of his Hamlet—

> In the fine soliloquy "O that this too, too solid flesh would
> melt," Garrick is completely overpowered by the tears of just
> grief for a virtuous father. . . . Of the words "so excellent a
> king," the last word is quite inaudible; you only perceive it by
> the motion of the mouth, which closes immediately afterwards
> firmly, and trembling with agitation as if to repress with his lips
> the only too clear indication of the grief which might unman
> him. This way of shedding tears, which shows the whole burden
> of inward grief, as well as the manly soul suffering under it,
> carries one irresistibly away.

So also with Garrick's Lear, which he played, it is to be
remembered, without a beard, and looking not like Elijah
but like John Wesley. Of this O'Keefe, the dramatist, said in
his *Recollections*—

> I liked him best in Lear. His saying in the bitterness of his
> anger, "I will do such things—what they are I know not," and
> his sudden recollection of his own want of power, were so pitiable
> as to touch the heart of every spectator. The simplicity of his
> saying, "Be these tears wet?—yes, faith," putting his finger to the
> cheek of Cordelia, and then looking at his finger, was exquisite.

Lessing and Romance

With the coming of Garrick, to be followed by Siddons and
Kemble, and then Edmund Kean and Macready, criticism
tended in England, during the second half of the eighteenth
century and the beginning of the nineteenth, to become a
chorus of praise, or, at least, of analytical observations about
the great actor or actress of the time being. Nothing was done
in England to correspond with the creative work of Lessing,
who "gave Goethe to Germany," and whose own lively and
forceful personality shines through every page he wrote.
The so-called "romantic movement," which he is credited
with having started, was, of course, not necessarily towards
romance in the medieval sense, but towards the enfranchise-
ment of imagination in every direction. He himself helped
to found German comedy in *Minna von Barnhelm*. What really
happened was very largely the discovery of Shakespeare and

of the new world and new impulse that he brought, and still brings, to each generation. It is, as I have striven to show, not merely romance that is his magic, but an ideal of humanity expressed within the Elizabethan patterns of art and society through which he had to work. At the touch of Shakespeare came the response of awakening genius in Goethe and Schiller, as in France later on in Victor Hugo and de Musset. But how different they all were, both from him and from each other!

Diderot's "Paradoxe"

Nor did any English critic achieve the practical effect of Lessing's French contemporary, Diderot. From the purely technical point of view, Diderot's famous *Paradoxe sur le Comédien*, and its study of real emotion in the mind of the actor, leads to pedantry in criticism when it is overdone. Everybody who has acted, even as an amateur, knows that one's mind is a mush of all sorts of conscious and subconscious experience and effort. By habit and imaginative concentration an actor can work an emotional force not only up to but far beyond his personal capacities in that direction. Diderot's basing of an argument on Garrick's casual gamut of grimaces is exploiting an after-dinner triviality beyond its value; but when Garrick cried on the stage as Hamlet or Lear before the public and for money he probably put into it the instinctive expression of every real-life emotion of the kind that occurred to him, as well as all he had rehearsed and imagined. He may at the same time have been quite conscious of a flickering wick among the primitive "floats" of his time.

Experience shows that when the character to be played coincides, however vaguely, with some intense experience in the actor's own life, sheer habit prompts both the method and force of the expression. We may be certain that Kean put into his Shylock—consciously or no—an enormous deal of the emotions of outraged pride that had tormented him in his forlorn years as he tramped from barn to barn. But this did not prevent him from thinking out every gesture, accent, and suggestion of character, and carrying the emotion through in the framework of his plan.

This kind of thing just fills up the crannies of criticism. Diderot's real value to the French stage was that, both as dramatist and critic, he helped to introduce there the drama of current middle-class life—the *tragédie bourgeoise* and the *comédie larmoyante*. This was already popular in England, where, as we have seen, it had been the bequest of Shirley and Heywood long before. It was to be the forbear of the middle-class comedy of Augier and Ohnet, of "drawing-room drama" and "Sardoodledom," ultimately of the Dumasian problem-play, which was never without its emotional side, of the domestic realism of Ibsen himself, of Chekhov's Russian ironies, and altogether of at least three-quarters of modern comedy and drama. On this side of the Channel, the importance of the actor and actress seemed to blind our critics to almost everything else that was happening. Neither Goldsmith's *She Stoops to Conquer* nor Sheridan's *The Rivals* was hailed with anything like a corresponding achievement in criticism. Not long ago, on looking up the contemporary notice of *The Rivals* in *The Morning Post*, of which I was the last critic, I found just a paragraph to the effect that it was a failure on its first performance and was being rewritten to suit the actors!

Siddons

One reason for concentration upon acting may have been that, since the reign of Garrick, the stage and auditorium had become divided into different worlds. Though there was still something of an "apron" to the stage, and stage-boxes and proscenium-doors were to survive even to the present day, the stage had now acquired an atmosphere of comparative mystery. The audience was kept not only off the stage but as far as possible on its own side of the curtain. Though it was not until the coming of gas that the lighting could be controlled, the very darkness of the stage could be, and was, used with haunting effect. So there came into being a new element of glamour—an appeal to the imagination which was all to the greater glory of the player.

This was the new theatre to which the majesty of Siddons appealed as something superhuman. With a reversal of mood not rare in London's theatrical history, the next morning's

papers raved over her return in 1782, as Isabella in Southerne's
The Fatal Marriage, to the Drury Lane she had left as an igno-
minious failure six years before. Far the best account of those
early performances of Siddons is the article written in *The
English Review* on all the characters of her first season. It was
by Thomas Holcroft, the shoe-maker's son from St. Martin's,
who was to go over to Paris and memorize *The Marriage of
Figaro* in the following year, to be imprisoned and very nearly
hanged for his Republican tendencies, but none the less to
become the author of *The Road to Ruin* and of *A Tale of Mystery*,
the first melodrama, of the old half-operatic style, to be
produced in this country. Holcroft's reasoned appreciation is
obviously trustworthy. He tells us that Siddons, whose personality was to become above all things regal and awe-inspiring,
impressed him then by her naturalness—

> No studied trick or start can be predicted, no forced tremula-
> tion, where the vacancy of the eye declares the absence of passion,
> can be seen; no laborious strainings at false climax, in which the
> tired voice reiterates one high tone beyond which it cannot
> reach, can be heard; no artificial heaving of the breasts, so dis-
> gusting when the affectation is perceptible—none of those arts
> by which the actress is seen and not the character—can be found
> in Mrs. Siddons. So natural are her gradations and transitions,
> so classical and correct her speech and deportment, and so
> exceedingly affecting and pathetical are her voice, form and
> features, that there is no conveying an idea of the pleasure she
> communicates by words. . . . She copies no-one, living or
> dead, but acts from nature and herself.

Edmund Kean

With the entry of Edmund Kean into Drury Lane on that
immortal January night of snow and slush in 1814, first-night
criticism counted for more than it had ever done before and,
perhaps, since. Wretched though the audience was, the critics
were there, and, among them, William Hazlitt of *The Morning
Chronicle*. One might almost say: "For Kean see Hazlitt."
Indeed, with or without Kean, there is hardly a single play of
Shakespeare regarding which a young critic cannot take down
his Hazlitt with advantage, and find something to start off
with. He may disagree with it; but how helpful the chance of
saying so! Upon Kean himself, Hazlitt's view is not always

borne out by other observers. Here, for instance, is what he says about Kean's Richard III—

> Mr. Kean's manner of acting this part has one peculiar advantage; it is entirely his own, without any traces of imitation of any other actor. . . . The opening scene, in which Richard descants on his own deformity, was conceived with perfect truth of character, and delivered in a fine and natural tone of varied recitation. . . . The concluding scene, in which he is killed by Richmond was the most brilliant. He fought like one drunk with wounds. The attitude in which he stands with his hands stretched out, after his sword is taken from him, has a preternatural and terrific grandeur, as if his will could not be disarmed, and the very phantoms of his despair had a withering power.

A few days later, Crabb Robinson of *The Times*, who happened to be a forbear of my own, and whose opinions were freely expressed to my parents over Crabb's breakfast-table in Russell Square, saw Kean in the same character. His absolutely candid diary gives an impression which is, in several matters, the direct contrary of Hazlitt's. On 7th March, 1814, he writes—

> At Drury Lane and saw Kean for the first time. He played Richard, I believe, better than any man I ever saw; yet my expectations were pitched too high, and I had not the pleasure I expected. The expression of malignant joy is the one in which he surpasses all men I have ever seen. His most flagrant defect is want of dignity. His face is finely expressive, though his mouth is not handsome, and he projects his lower lip ungracefully. . . . He satisfied my eye more than my ear.
>
> His action was very often that of Kemble, and this was not the worst of his performance; but it detracts from his past boasted originality. His declamation is very unpleasant, but my ear may in time be reconciled to it, as the palate is to new cheese and tea. His speech is not fluent, and his words and syllables are too distinctly separated. . . . The concluding scene was unequal to my expectation. He did not often excite a strong persuasion of the truth in his acting, and the applause he received was not very great. . . . I do not think he will retain all his popularity; but he may learn to deserve it better.

Lamb's "The Old Actors"

A remarkable thing is that the greatest genius among the London critics of that time, who lived through the careers of both Siddons and Kean and must have seen both of them constantly, gives us practically no declared reminiscence of them. Charles Lamb chose his own themes. They belonged to another world than that of the theatrical news of his day. The "Mr. K." and "Mrs. S." who occur as side-glance illustrations of his "Essay on the Tragedies of Shakespeare" leave not much doubt of their identity; but it would seem the very fame of these players convinced him, not rightly perhaps, that the greater tragedies are at their best acted by the imagination of the reader at his fireside. If Lamb had set out to be logical—and Heaven forfend he should ever have done that!—he would have remembered that everyone had not got his imagination. Other people's minds were not, as his was, stored with memories of performances on the stage, which he could improve upon in his thoughts. But the immediate traffic of criticism was not Lamb's affair. He "wrote for antiquity." As a matter of fact he was for a fortnight my predecessor—on trial as dramatic critic of *The Morning Post*. He was not given the position, though he continued to supply jokes.

The performances he recalled afterwards—"The Old Actors" and "The Artificial Comedy of the Last Century"—were so far away when he wrote about them that they were hardly real at all. Yet he has made them much more vivid and beautiful things to us than many current productions which we saw yesterday or the day before. They live and move still before our eyes—Munden "wondering, like primeval man with the sun and stars about him"; Dicky Suett, with is "O La!" the "gay boldness of Jack Palmer as Joseph Surface; old Dodd and Miss Pope," the perfect gentlewoman.

These bright figures that rustle and sparkle through Lamb's essays would be vulgarized and spoiled only if one thought for a moment that they were human players over whom another critic might differ, or who would be likely to demand a rise in salary on the score of a "good press." I like to think of them as pure inventions of Lamb's own—appropriate products of the relief he so bravely sought from an always imminent sorrow by keeping a kind of old curiosity-shop in the background of his fancy. They are his dream-friends, of whom he cannot believe that the comedy they played was intended to have anything so solid as a moral purpose—though most assuredly

it was. With all their complete incorrectness as workaday
models, it is possible that those essays of Charles Lamb have
made more people love the theatre than any criticism that has
ever been written. They are also profoundly if not commercially
true. The more one sees of plays, the more one is bound to
realize that "these our actors are all spirits." What is real to
them is unreal to us. Their effect upon us is all that we share.
They must pass and have their day. Only the idea of them,
which is the critic's merchandise, and sometimes the play
itself remain.

Leigh Hunt

Though he was six years younger than Hazlitt, and nine
years younger than Lamb, Leigh Hunt could probably claim
to be, as William Archer describes him in the introduction to
Dramatic Essays, "the first English dramatic critic." This is
in the sense that he was the "first writer of any note who made
it his business to see and report upon all the principal theatrical
events of the day." As a boy of 19 he became dramatic
critic of his brother's daily paper, *The News*—transferring three
years after to his own paper, *The Examiner*, of which he was
dramatic critic for five years. Then came a gap of seventeen
years, after which for a year and five months he wrote the
entire four pages of his own unsuccessful daily paper, *The
Tatler*, in which dramatic criticisms were the chief feature.

In the arduous circumstances, one should, perhaps, forgive
Hunt for proving sometimes distinctly tame in comparison
with Lamb, and even with Hazlitt. He made it his confessed
aim to be "nothing if not critical." He failed to consecrate
"the grins of Munden" with fancies of his own. But, considering his youth, the notices in *The News* are remarkably well-
written and perceptive. His *Autobiography*, too, gives an entertaining as well as instructive picture of the state of affairs
prevailing between press and theatre in the early days of the
nineteenth century. At certain points, something not altogether
different from the present paragraphist's world seems to be
suggested—

Puffing and plenty of tickets were the system of the day. It
was an interchange of amenities over the dinner-table; a flattery

of power on the one side, and puns on the other; and what the
public took for a criticism on a play was a draft upon the box-office,
or reminiscences of last Thursday's salmon and lobster-sauce.
The custom was to write as short and favourable a paragraph
on the new piece as could be; to say, that Bannister was "excellent" and Mrs. Jordan "charming"; to notice the "crowded
house," or invent it, if necessary; and to conclude by observing
that "the whole went off with *éclat*." A critical religion in those
times was to admire Mr. Kemble; and at the period in question
Master Betty had appeared and been hugged to the hearts of the
town as the "young Roscius."

It is to Leigh Hunt's honour that, in spite of his youth and
inexperience, he stood out against all this. He did his best to
treat the drama seriously as an art. He was independent,
even to the extent of getting his brother to pay for the paper's
ticket to the theatre. The result was, as he himself tells us, that
his views came to be respected far beyond the value even he
put upon them.

Mrs. Inchbald

While Lamb and Hazlitt and Leigh Hunt enjoy their deserved
prominence in the critical firmament, it is only fair that we
should pay a certain special tribute of memory to one of their
feminine contemporaries—Elizabeth Inchbald, actress, novelist,
playwright, editress, and charming woman. She may not have
been actually the first woman-critic. Mrs. Aphra Behn had
done something of the kind. But Mrs. Behn did not leave behind
anything like the survey of the entire dramatic literature of
her period which Mrs. Inchbald did. Nor did she view the
theatre in the same enlightening way from a Regency gentlewoman's standpoint of morals and manners. In my book,
Elizabeth Inchbald and Her Circle, I had the pleasure of paying
such tribute as I could to the delightful personality of this
Norfolk farmer's daughter, who shared Siddons's early priva-
tions—including a dinner off raw turnips in a field—and lived
to become the adored "little old lady" of Drury Lane, keeping
her dairymaid-duchess prettiness and her self-respect to the
last.

Her critical fame will rest upon the task set her by Longman

of editing—or, at any rate, writing prefaces to—his edition of
The British Theatre. The main difference between Mrs.
Inchbald's criticisms and those which a modern critic would
write is that she hardly worried at all about truth to life. It
was far more important that the moral should be "just"—that
it should coincide with a certain scheme of desirability which
no one of that period dreamed of living up to. Also it was
demanded that the manners of all except the low-comedy
scenes should be "elegant." Given these essentials, all was
well. If by any chance there should be introduced any
single character which could be described as "new to the
stage," this was an occasion for something very like genuine
excitement.

"Speed the Plough"

Upon the score of "decorum in love," Mrs. Inchbald objects to
Morton's racy, rural comedy, *Speed the Plough*, which introduced
Mrs. Grundy to the world. Here the heroine falls in love
with the squire's son disguised as a ploughman. That this
should happen offended Mrs. Inchbald to the quick. She could
only understand it on the assumption that "some preternatural
agent whispered that he was a man of birth." In any case she
preferred to impute the cause of this sudden passion to some
"magical information," conveyed either by "the palpitation of
the heart, or the quickness of the eye," rather than to the
"want of female refinement."

She damns with very faint praise the simplicities of that
estimable, if ponderous, homily in homespun, *George Barnwell*,
with its story of the once-hopeful apprentice who became a
thief and a murderer through the allurements of a light-o'-love.
"It has been popular," she confesses, but "revived notions of
elegance in calamity have, in late times, reduced the play to a
mere holiday performance." It was, of course, habitually
produced at Christmas before the pantomime, and "guyed"
by a noisy and impatient audience. Concerning Mrs. Inchbald's Shakespearian criticism one can speak in little else but
terms of apology. She simply did not understand Shakespeare.
His bold fancy and free humanity were too wholly at variance
with the traditions of her time.

Women-dramatists

When it comes to the tradition of gay, bustling comedies which did survive amidst the eighteenth century's banal sentiments and glamorous terrors, Mrs. Inchbald knew everything there was to know. Without a trace of jealousy, she praises the plays written by other women-dramatists. In her age they were a comparatively new thing. She was born only eighty years after the death of Aphra Behn, the "George Sand of the Restoration" and undoubted pioneer in England of the play-writing sisterhood. The interval is almost exactly filled up by two other women-playwrights. One was Mrs. Centlivre, authoress of *The Busybody*, adapted from Molière's *L'Étourdi*, and also of that admirable acting-comedy, *The Wonder: A Woman Keeps a Secret*. The other was Mrs. Cowley, the "Anna Matilda" of the Della Cruscans and authoress of *The Belle's Stratagem*, in the first production of which, at Covent Garden, Mrs. Inchbald herself had appeared.

So far as Aphra Behn is concerned, Mrs. Inchbald could not do anything in particular, for the simple reason that Mrs. Behn's plays, though brisk and witty, were hardly of the kind a lady could praise. True, the worst that Aphra Behn wrote was not nearly so vile as the things that were written about her. Mrs. Centlivre is different. She, too, is credited with some gay adventures, but she had the advantage of being married to Queen Anne's cook. Mrs. Inchbald launches into fearless encomiums of her. There is no question as to a happy idea lurking behind each of Mrs. Centlivre's comedies. *A Bold Stroke for a Wife*, with its skit upon Quakers, has enriched our language with "the real Simon Pure." Garrick's choice of the part of Don Felix in *The Wonder* as that in which he should bid farewell to the stage was by no means an unworthy honour to the "wrangling-lovers scene." Mrs. Cowley, though *The Belle's Stratagem* was to hold the stage longer than anything by Mrs. Centlivre, had less genius than the other two. Her efforts at tragedy were anything but triumphs. One of them, *The Fate of Sparta*, called forth a famous epigram from Parsons, the actor—

> Ingenious Cowley, while we viewed
> Of Sparta's sons the lot severe,

> We caught the Spartan fortitude,
> And saw their woes without a tear.

Farces

In spite of Mrs. Cowley's limitations—and although, as a younger rival, Mrs. Inchbald might have had some excuse for mentioning them—she finds, as a critic, only what is good. Still more in her *Collection of Farces*, published some three years after, Mrs. Inchbald holds a ground upon which modernity cannot challenge her. We have grown accustomed to elaborate and highly-mechanized three-act farce—the type which Sir Arthur Pinero brought to perfection—and we have farces of ideas, like *The Importance of Being Earnest* or *Fanny's First Play*. But we have nothing which corresponds to the short, free-and-easy farce of character, with or without songs, in which the eighteenth century revelled. For this reason, if for no other, it is worth while to turn over some of these old pages even now. One does not find great literature. One does not find what we should call careful dramatic joinery or playcraft. But, in such farces as *The Devil to Pay*, *No Song No Supper*, *Raising the Wind*, and a host of others, there was an irreplaceable rough-and-tumble spirit, and at the same time an appetite for characters. The nearest we can get is in revue and broadcast sketches. It was no mere accident that Dickens in his youth devoured Mrs. Inchbald's *Farces*, and confessed afterwards how much he owed to them. Alfred Jingle, first cousin of Jeremy Diddler in *Raising the Wind*, was not the only Pickwickian who walked straight out of Mrs. Inchbald's pages to take on a new immortality.

CHAPTER IX

"HEROIC" AND OTHER VERSE

BEFORE we bid good-bye to the shallow artifice, forced sentiment, and false morality that contented Mrs. Inchbald in her graver moods, it may be well to turn back for a moment to something of which the afterglow was still lingering in her early days. I mean the old "heroic" drama of Dryden and his seventeenth-century friends and rivals. For serious dramatic purposes the "heroic" drama, with its conscious bombast, exotic themes, deeds of violence, and interminable love-and-honour debates in rhyming verse, spoken by gorgeous figures, plumed and periwigged, in front of gaudily conventional scenery, did not outlast the generation that gave it birth. Indeed, it actually flourished for little more than fifteen years. The "heroic" rhymed couplet, however, which was to so large an extent its signature, remained all through the eighteenth century the unchallenged vehicle of prologue, epilogue, and official theatrical utterances of every kind. It still lives in that most permanently popular of all forms of dramatic entertainment in England—the Christmas pantomime. Also, there is no kind of dramatic writing which has enshrined and inspired so much lively as well as forcible criticism.

Sir William Davenant

So far as drama was concerned there remains no doubt that the idea of the heroic rhymed play was brought over from France by Shakespeare's godson and reputed offspring, Sir William Davenant. His opera, *The Siege of Rhodes*, produced at Lincoln's Inn Fields in 1661, and in part at Rutland House before the Restoration, was—according to Professor Edward J. Dent in his *Foundations of British Opera*—originally written as a drama in rhymed heroic couplets in imitation of Corneille. Davenant had converted it into an opera just as a means of getting it presented at all, in view of the Puritan ban upon regular plays. At King Charles's suggestion, Orrery then tried his hand; but it was "glorious" John Dryden who was to be the heroic's supreme exponent and champion. In the prologue to *Secret Love, or The Maiden Queen* (1666) he makes no secret of his purpose or its source—

> He who writ this, not without pains and thought
> From French and English theatres has brought
> The exactest rules by which a play is wrought;
> The unities of action, place and time;
> The scenes unbroken and a mingled chime
> Of Jonson's humour, with Corneille's rhyme.

Just eleven years later, in the composition of his Antony-and-Cleopatra tragedy, *All for Love* (1677), a change of plan was to be announced. "In this" he tells us, "I have professed to imitate the divine Shakespeare, which that I might perform more freely, I have disencumbered myself from rhyme."

In the meantime, none the less, he had set an undoubted temporary vogue for the heroic with the success of *Tyrannick Love* (1669) and *The Conquest of Granada* (1670). In his *Essay of Heroic Plays* he showed frank satisfaction with the result—

> Whether heroic verse ought to be admitted into serious plays is not now to be disputed. 'Tis already in possession of the stage; and I dare confidently affirm that very few tragedies, in this age, shall be received without it.

Dryden's Decline

Even after *All For Love*, Dryden was to return to rhyme in *Aureng-Zebe*—his drama about the incestuous love-affairs of the contemporary Mogul emperor. The play was recently revived, but turned out a very poor and unconvincing museum-piece. In his prologue to it Dryden confessed that he was beginning to lose faith in his "long-loved mistress, rhyme," and to recognize that "passion's too fierce to be in fetters bound." Wisdom after the event suggests that if unbroken rhyme had been an ideal dramatic medium, Shakespeare, who started as an all-out rhymester, would not have gradually dropped it, as he did.

Possibly certain deficiencies in Dryden himself were partly to blame for the speedy fading-out of the heroic rhymed play. His virile and active mind expressed itself in many ways, including some of the best critical prose ever written. As a dramatist he is just a sometimes-magnificent workman. He knew all the models and technical tricks. He was alive to every movement of his day. He was a great journalist. He understood that what the little world of the Restoration theatre wanted at each point was something new and startling. The rules and rhymes from France appeared at the time fresh ideas. So, with the help of bombast, horrible scenes, unnatural crimes, and florid spectacles, the heroic play did for a time enjoy exciting response. But the vibration of moral and decorative extravagance against technical severity could not have lasted for long on its own account. Inevitably it grew stale.

Thomas Otway

To be sure, there was one dramatist of genius, Thomas Otway, who did come for a time under the influence of the rhymed heroic; but he soon threw it off for a return to the freedom of Elizabethan blank verse. He was also responsible for the arrival of an appeal of pathos and of simple human passion which gives, as none of Dryden's dramatic writing does, the impression of being part of himself.

With his customary candour, Dryden recognized that in these respects he was beaten by Otway. Though Otway had faults of his time, no tragic play of the period has gripped me with the emotional power of *Venice Preserved*—especially on its production by the Phoenix Society, with those two fine actors, the late Ion Swinley and Baliol Holloway as Pierre and Jaffier, and Cathleen Nesbitt as Belvidera. Here, instead of a mass of heroical rhodomontade, we have the definite clash of friendship and loyalty. With it was coupled the real, abject ardour of love that Otway himself had experienced, as we learn from his letters to Mrs. Barry, Lord Rochester's mistress, the beautiful but fickle actress for whom the character of Belvidera was written. Whether or not she drove Otway to his early and miserable death, he had the consolation of seeing her play his heroine. She did so, by all accounts, extremely well.

It is not our knowledge of Otway's hopeless attachment that matters. It is the fact that this inspires the play with a human truth and intensity which need no support either of spectacle or rhyme. So, too, in a smaller measure, with *The Orphan*, and its intimate contrast between sincerely-loved husband and lustful seducer. It is no matter for wonder that Otway's plays have lived consistently on the stage through nearly three centuries—an honour shared by neither Dryden's nor Lee's nor Orrery's, nor by those of any other of the heroic dramatists.

Satire

One curious reason hastened the decline of the heroic play. Though the rhymed couplet showed itself unsuitable and monotonous as the sole vehicle of serious English drama, it had proved—as it still proves, with its simple swing and counter-swing—exactly fitted for satire. It was, in fact, used superbly for that purpose by Dryden himself, as by every satirist from Pope to Byron, and on to the present day. It became not so much the language of drama as of criticism—and, above all, of that half-creative form of criticism, burlesque. Already, before Dryden's farewell to it in *Aureng-Zebe*, the rhymed couplet had been mercilessly turned back at the heroic play-wrights' heads in Buckingham's skit, *The Rehearsal*—now a surer and much more familiar classic than most of the plays it ridicules. Both its prologue and epilogue are sound and searching criticism in verse—

> Here brisk, insipid wits, for wit, let fall
> Sometimes dull sense, but oftener none at all.
> There strutting heroes, with a grim-faced train,
> Shall brave the gods in King Cambyses's vein.
> For (changing rules of late, as if men writ
> In spite of reason, nature, art and wit,)
> Our poets make us laugh at tragedy
> And with their comedies they make us cry . . .
> Wherefore, for ours and for the kingdom's peace,
> May this prodigious way of writing cease;
> Let's have, at least once in our lives, a time
> When we may hear some reason, not all rhyme.

After this, not to mention *The Rehearsal* itself, with its bibulous Kings of Brentford and the wordy prowess of Drawcansir, who boasted that he "slew both friend and foe," one can understand even Dryden recognizing that fashion had changed, and that the hour for forsaking his "long-loved mistress" for good was drawing near.

Rhetoric

The value of the heroic for prologue, epilogue, and any lightly sententious or satirical rhetoric, had been, of course, shown long before even the arrival of the heroic play. Ben Jonson, though he abjured it for plays themselves even more readily than Shakespeare, was a master of the heroic rhyme for other purposes—as his immortal tribute to the "Swan of Avon" proves well enough. His prologue to *Every Man in his Humour* is a vigorous assertion of his purpose as the writer of a comedy of humours. It is also an invaluable sidelight upon the drawbacks of the sort of stage that he and Shakespeare had known. He bade his audience see a play—

> as other plays should be,
> Where neither chorus wafts you o'er the seas
> Nor creaking throne comes down the boys to please:
> Nor nimble squib is seen to make afeard
> The gentlewoman; nor rolled bullet heard
> To say, it thunders; nor tempestuous drum
> Rumbles to tell you when the storm doth come;
> But deeds and language such as men do use,
> And persons such as comedy would choose,
> When she would show an image of the times,
> And sport with human folly, not with crimes.

How much of the success of *Tyrannic Love* was due, one wonders, to Dryden's own brilliant and ever-famous epilogue "spoken by Nell Gwynn, when she was to be carried off dead by the Bearers." Certainly it is more universally remembered than anything in the play itself, and gives one a better idea of Nell Gwynn's personality, through her own mouth, than any chronicle—

> Hold! Are you mad, you damned, confounded dog?
> I am to rise and speak the epilogue . . .
> I come, kind gentlemen, strange news to tell ye;
> I am the ghost of poor, departed Nelly.
> Sweet ladies, be not frighted, I'll be civil;
> I'm what I was, a little, harmless devil . . .
> As for my epitaph, when I am gone,

> I'll trust no poet, but will write my own.
> "Here Nelly lies, who, though she lived a slattern,
> Yet died a princess, acting in St. Catherine!"

Some peculiarly vivid impressions of the Restoration audience as they appeared to the actor, actress, and dramatist can be got from these prologues and epilogues of the late seventeenth century. They have one merit above the more polished addresses of the eighteenth—they did not treat their "friends in front" to the fulsome flattery which grew so tedious later on, or make appeals to pity or forbearance. All through them one feels that players and authors alike despised their public. They had, apparently every reason to do so. Here, for instance, are the last lines of Mrs. Aphra Behn's almost savage prologue to her play, *The Rover, or The Banished Cavaliers*. Whether any of its hearers recognized themselves or no is not recorded—

> The younger sparks who hither do resort
> Cry, "Pox o' your gentle things! Give us more sport." . . .
> Such fops are never pleased unless the play
> Be stuffed with fools as brisk and dull as they.
> Such might the half-crown spare, and in a glass
> At home behold a more accomplished ass;
> Where they may set their cravats, wigs and faces,
> And practice all their buffoon'ry grimaces—
> "See how this huff becomes—this damme stare!"—
> Which they at home may act because they dare . . .
> O that our Nokes, our Tony Lee, could show
> A fop but half so much to th' life as you!

The Wit of Garrick

The most prolific and lively of all heroic prologue-writers was undoubtedly Garrick. He knew exactly what his actors and actresses—and he himself—could do to get the audience into a good humour. What sly and sparkling touches Mrs. Abingdon must have put into that epilogue he wrote for her to give a comic finish to Murphy's tragedy of *Zenobia*! Still more, what easy mastery of character, both as author and as actor, must have been behind Garrick's own appearances in his own prologues—as, say, the "Country Boy" who heralded Brown's *Barbarossa* by looking for his "measter" in the pit and gallery, or as the "Sailor (fuddled)" who came on singing

"How pleasant a sailor's life passes" in front of *The Mask of Britannia*! From a critical point of view one of the most incisive and informative of the Garrick prologues was that spoken by himself in front of Whitehead's *The School for Lovers*. He was supposed to be recounting a talk with the author—

> "Not change your scenes?" said I,—I'm sorry for't;
> My constant friends above, around, below,
> Have English tastes, and love both change and show;
> Without such aid even Shakespeare would be flat,
> Our crowded pantomimes are proof of that.
> What eager transport starts from every eye,
> When pullies rattle and our genii fly!
> When tin cascades, like falling waters gleam,
> And through the canvas bursts the real stream;
> While thirsty Islington laments, in vain,
> Half her New River rolled to Drury Lane!
> "Lord, Sir," said I, "for gallery, boxes, pit,
> I'll back my Harlequin against your wit."
> Yet still the author, anxious for his play,
> Shook his wise head—"What will the critics say?"
> "As usual, Sir, abuse you all they can?"
> "And what the ladies?"—"He's a charming man!
> A charming piece!—One scarce knows what it means;
> But that's no matter when there's such sweet scenes."

Dr. Johnson's Masterpiece

One can understand how effective all this must have been when it was Garrick who spoke it. It reveals still a popular taste in Garrick's time not altogether different from tendencies perceptible nowadays—in spite of the rivalry of television and the cinema. But Garrick's prologues grew more and more to rely on the actor or the actress. They did not survive on the strength of their own ring of phrase and precision of thought, as did those of his old friend and instructor, Dr. Johnson. The prologue Johnson wrote for the opening of Drury Lane under Garrick's and Lacy's management in 1747 remains the unchallengeable masterpiece in its own kind. Here were dignity blended with wit, satire as agreeably free from spite as from remorse, a critical history of our stage condensed into a few minutes' utterance, a theatrical philosophy at once concise and unanswerable. The opening lines about Shakespeare and "panting Time" have become so hackneyed that people are

apt to forget how much else there is in that "copy of verses."
How true, even now, the couplet upon Ben Jonson's fate!—

> Cold approbation gave the lingering bays,
> For those who durst not censure scarce could praise.

Almost as true—and not less sacrificially candid, for there
was much in Dryden that Johnson regarded with almost
religious reverence—was his view of "the wits of Charles,"
whose "reign was long," till "virtue called oblivion to her aid."
Not least, there is hardly a single actor or servant of the "many-
headed" master who would not still subscribe to Johnson's
ultimate concession—

> Hard is his lot that, here by fortune placed,
> Must watch the wild vicissitudes of taste:
> With every meteor of caprice must play,
> And chase the new-blown bubble of the day.
> Ah, let not censure term our fate our choice,
> The stage but echoes back the public voice;
> The drama's laws the drama's patrons give,
> For we that live to please must please to live.

Churchill's "Rosciad"

From a purely critical view not many efforts in heroic rhyme
of that age can vie in force and genuine value with Churchill's
Rosciad. For all its unflinching candour in regard to the
eighteenth-century stage, it was by no means altogether unfair.
One need not wonder at its bringing sudden fame and the
beginning of what might have been fortune to the obscure
curate of St. John's, Westminster. It is not merely a satire.
Churchill gives even to his most ruthless caricatures a touch of
portraiture that makes them live. Even for the victim himself,
it was an achievement to have inspired such lines as these
upon Quin—

> His eyes in gloomy socket taught to roll,
> Proclaimed the sullen 'habit of the soul':
> Heavy and phlegmatic he trod the stage,
> Too proud for tenderness, too dull for rage.
> When Hector's lovely widow shines in tears,
> Or Rowe's gay rake dependent virtue jeers,
> With the same cast of features he is seen
> To chide the libertine and court the queen . . .

> In whate'er cast his character was laid
> Self still, like oil, upon the surface played.
> Nature, in spite of all his skill, crept in:
> Horatio, Dorax, Falstaff—still 'twas Quin.

What dramatic pungency he gives to his description of Barry as Hamlet, at the time when the ghost of "buried Denmark" is just about to appear!—

> Some dozen lines before the Ghost is there,
> Behold him for the solemn scene prepare;
> See how he frames his eyes, poses each limb,
> Puts the whole body into proper trim—
> From whence we learn, with no great stretch of art,
> Five lines hence comes a ghost—and Ha! a start!

It is to Churchill's credit that, whatever his faults as a man and as an ordained minister of religion, he was absolutely honest as a critic. He gave unstinted praise where he felt it deserved, as with Kitty Clive and Mrs. Cibber and Garrick. He was prepared to take without flinching whatever attacks his judgments brought about. In his *Apology* he defends his method with vigour against critics who seem to have been just as abusive but less ingenuous—

> A critic was of old a glorious name,
> Whose sanction handed merit up to fame;
> Beauties as well as faults he brought to view,
> His judgment great, and great his candour, too;
> No servile rules drew sickly taste aside;
> Secure he walked, for Nature was his guide.
> But now—O, strange reverse!—our critics bawl
> In praise of candour with a heart of gall;
> Conscious of guilt, and fearful of the light,
> They lurk enshrouded in the veil of night;
> Safe from detection, seize the unwary prey,
> And stab, like bravoes, all who come that way.

Fading Fashion

After Johnson, the fine flavour of prologue and epilogue began to be less conspicuous. Though Sheridan wrote some, his wit did not shine between the formal ding-dongs of heroic verse. It needed the free rhythm of that scintillating prose over which his mastery was unrivalled. There was another reason, too. It is explained in the prologue—which Sheridan himself

did not write—to *The Critic*, his delightful adaptation of the
idea of *The Rehearsal* to a new theme and another age. This
reason was (as the Hon. Richard Fitzpatrick, the prologue's
author, tells us) that the plays themselves were less inspiring
even to satire—

> In those gay days of wickedness and wit,
> When Villiers criticized what Dryden writ,
> The tragic queen, to please a tasteless crowd,
> Had learned to bellow, rant and roar so loud,
> That frightened Nature, her best friend before,
> The blustering beldam's company forswore . . .
> The frantic hero's wild delirium past,
> Now insipidity succeeds bombast;
> So slow Melpomene's cold numbers creep,
> Here dulness seems her drowsy court to keep.

So prologue and epilogue faded out—partly through sheer
inanition, and partly through the arrival of a new and less
intimate public, without either technical or traditional knowledge of the stage, upon whom adroit allusion would be naturally
wasted. Another change that has to be reckoned was brought
about by gas. This made the turning down of the lights in the
auditorium a sufficient hint that the play was starting. In
times when the house-lights had to be on all the while a definite
occurrence was needed, beyond the stoppage of the orchestra
(if any) and the three knocks, to mark the opening and to get
the audience into listening trim.

Whether something in the nature of a prologue should be
generally revived or not is a question that has often been raised.
The answer is that where there is no need there is no time.
As things are, most plays on their first night are so late in
beginning that everybody who really cares is impatient for
the curtain to rise upon the opening scene, and at the finish
most people want to get off as quickly as ever they can. For
gala occasions we still have prologues—generally in the old
rhymed heroic—and in revue the compère does his duty in
giving a rough idea of anything we ought, or ought not, to
know beforehand.

Undoubtedly modern stage-management does not always
cope with possibilities at curtain-fall as fully as it might. At
times one feels that a written epilogue would be happier than

the often feeble impromptus of the leading man or leading lady—not to say the entire cast and the author himself. The trouble would be, of course, that, if there were a written epilogue, the personal receptions afterwards would still be called for, and probably responded to. The best way out seems to be just for someone to prepare three speeches very carefully —one in case of obvious failure, one in case of triumphant success, and one in case of a half-and-half verdict which has got to be made to appear like a success. The last of them is, of course, the only one that really matters—and it does matter a very great deal!

Burlesque

But, though prologue and epilogue passed away, the old heroic lived on. It was welcomed to a new home, in which it could be found flourishing honourably very nearly a hundred years after—in burlesque. Beyond all question it had a magical effect upon that ancient form of comedy, which goes back not merely to Aristophanes, but to Susarion and the old satyric dances of Greece, and to recitals of the mock-Homeric poem, *Batrachomyomachia,* recounting the Battle of the Frogs and Mice. Perhaps the peculiar fitness of the heroic line for burlesque was the actual result of its unsuitability to the tragedies for which it had been used. Its lack of variety and of lift, and its pompous restriction of all expression to direct antitheses were exactly right for the conveyance of punning phrases and immediate contrasts between the sublime and the ridiculous.

Until its arrival—so far as our English stage was concerned— written burlesque or extravaganza as a definite form of drama-tic parody was comparatively rare. Shakespeare only gave us snatches, like the clowns' play in *A Midsummer Night's Dream.* For modern purposes, Beaumont's and Fletcher's *The Knight of the Burning Pestle* is generally counted the pioneer, with its Don Quixote satire in Ralph, the romance-struck grocer's apprentice, whom Mr. Noel Coward played so memorably as a young actor of twenty in the Kingsway revival. But *The Knight of the Burning Pestle* is at the heart of it a comedy of real characters. Its scenes of parody arrive only incident-ally. Even *The Rehearsal,* like *The Critic,* which was to follow it after just over a century, was a comedy with burlesque-interludes.

"Tom Thumb the Great"

The first full-blown modern burlesque, beginning and ending as a parody, was to come almost exactly between them. It was Henry Fielding's *The Tragedy of Tragedies, or The Life and Death of Tom Thumb the Great.* The theatrical scholarship Fielding lavished upon that celebrated and once immensely popular work has its inevitable drawbacks for producing present-day laughter. So much of it relies upon a knowledge of long-forgotten originals—Dryden's *The Conquest of Granada*, Thomson's *Sophonisba*, Lee's *Mithridates*, Addison's *Cato*, and the rest. It is in some ways better to read than to see acted, because one can look at the parodied lines on the same page. Often they are just as ridiculous as the burlesque, and sometimes more so. But this "spotting" of sources is at the same time the death of true humour and of true perception. The best things in *Tom Thumb*, after all, are lines that have a touch beyond annotation, like the mock-simplicity of the famous mock-simile—

> So, when two dogs are fighting in the streets
> With a third dog one of the two dogs meets,
> With angry teeth he bites him to the bone,
> And this dog smarts for what that dog has done.

Far less subtle though it be, there is more of the broad slash of the kind of burlesque that survives its victims about *Chrononhotonthologos*, which arrived four years later and was by Henry Carey, author of "Sally in our Alley" and forbear of Edmund Kean. "Go call a coach and let a coach be called!" still rings in everybody's memory almost as surely as the old song that brought Carey his greater fame. The prologue, too, has a straightforward punch about it that Fielding's learned and allusive preface has perforce to forfeit—

> To-night our comic muse the buskin wears
> And gives herself no small romantic airs . . .
> In ridicule's strict retrospect displays
> The poetasters of these modern days,
> Who with big, bellowing bombast rend our ears,

> Which stript of sound quite void of sense appears;
> Or else their fiddle-faddle numbers flow,
> Serenely dull, elaborately low.

Another burlesque of the pre-punning period which can boast of lines that are classics on their own account was William Barnes Rhodes's *Bombastes Furioso*, first played at the Haymarket in 1810. It was a much cleverer little skit than its comparative neglect suggests. The first words of Fusbos, Minister to Artaxominous the Great, King of Utopia, have always seemed to me a particularly neat hit at the courtly familiarities prevailing in romantic plays even within memory—

> Hail, Artaxominous, y'clept "the Great"!
> I come, an humble pillar of thy state,
> Pregnant with news—but, ere that news I tell,
> First let me hope your Majesty is well.

Nor should the succinct finality of Bombastes's epitaph go without recognition—

> Here lies Bombastes, stout of heart and limb,
> Who conquered all but Fusbos—Fusbos him.

James Robinson Planché

Among other distinctions, *Bombastes Furioso* can claim to have inspired James Robinson Planché, creator of nineteenth-century extravaganza, to his first effort, *Amoroso, King of Little Britain*, written originally for amateurs and presented at Drury Lane in 1818. "If a pun be a crime," Planché was a master of criminals. There were worse punsters to follow; but Planché started the whole school that kept the "sacred lamp of burlesque" continuously alight from the production of his *Olympic Revels*, at the now-vanished Olympic Theatre in 1831, to the 1895 revival of *Little Jack Sheppard*. This was the last flicker of the Gaiety tradition, to be immediately followed by the arrival of George Edwardes's invention of musical comedy, represented by *The Shop Girl*. Throughout his long life—he died in 1880 at the age of 84—Planché remained faithful and prolific. Among his rivals and successors were Gilbert a' Beckett, Mark Lemon, the future Sergeant Talfourd, Robert and William Brough, W. S. (afterwards Sir William)

Gilbert, Albert Smith, Shirley Brooks, Tom Taylor, F. C. (afterwards Sir Francis) Burnand, H. J. Byron, and Robert Reece. Thanks to these and others, every conceivable subject in tragedy, opera, classical mythology, current melodrama, and children's fairy-tale found itself honoured at one or other of the half-dozen theatres where burlesque and extravaganza were a regular part of the bill of fare in Victorian days. The burlesques took all sorts of forms: some of the early ones were one-act, inexpensive affairs, included in a varied dramatic programme before or after the drama. When George Edwardes joined John Hollingshead at the Gaiety they began to be long, three-act spectacles costing a fortune. But right to the finish the rhymed heroic verse and the pun were characteristics common to all.

About Victorian burlesque and extravaganza in its palmy days were certain merits which compare by no means unfavourably with the taste and tenor of much present-day entertainment. It was written by educated people mainly for educated people. It did not just harp stupidly upon physical sensations, or allow its concessions to ignorance to paralyse all fancy. Though it was thoroughly human, intelligent allusions were possible. In his *Book of Burlesque*, Davenport Adams emphasizes this—

> Modern burlesque was fortunate indeed in its founders—all of them men of letters as well as playwrights. . . . They came fresh to the task and made the most of their opportunities. They set themselves really to travesty and to parody, and were careful to present, amid their wildest comicalities, a definite, intelligible story. They dropped naturally into the decasyllabic couplet, and made free use of the pun; but in neither case did they become mechanical or strained. The verse of Planché and Beckett is smoothness itself, and they do not descend to word-torturing. Talfourd and the Broughs took more licence in this respect; but they never sank to drivel. Above all, not one of these masters of burlesque permitted himself to be vulgar either in general treatment or in verbal detail. They were nice in their choice of subjects, and, like W. S. Gilbert in the case of *The Princess*, perverted them respectfully.

By way of example, here is a speech from Planché's second burlesque—*Olympic Devils*, a sequel to *Olympic Revels*—daring

to treat of the Greek Fates with a wit and grace and cultured
understanding quite outside the apparent scope of the average
jazz-band crooner and "boobadoop" comedian now prevalent—

> I vow you fates are most industrious spinsters!
> Miss Clotho there—man's destiny beginning—
> Life's thread at tea, like a tee-totum, spinning.
> And then Miss Lachesis that same thread measures,
> Taking great pains, but giving little pleasures.
> Last comes Miss Atropos, her part fulfilling,
> And cuts poor mortals off without a shilling.
> The saddest sister of the fatal three,
> Daughter, indeed, of shear necessity!
> Plying her awful task with due decorum,
> A never-ceasing game of "snip-snap-snorum"!
> For help—alas!—man pleads to her in vain—
> Her motto's "Cut and never come again."

Extravaganza

Strangely enough, Planché's first big success in fairy extravaganza, *Riquet with the Tuft*—taken, like *Cinderella*, *Puss in
Boots*, *Blue-beard*, and *The Sleeping Beauty*, from old Perrault—
is almost the only theme of his that has never been repeated.
Yet how charming a story it tells, of the ugly but witty prince
and the beautiful but stupid princess, and of how the prince
was suddenly transformed into a handsome man and the princess began to say clever and delightful things!   According to
Perrault's "moral," the transformation was due to the magic
of love. There was no real alteration; but the prince suddenly
appeared to be handsome and the princess's conversation to be
engaging. This would, of course, never do for extravaganza
purposes.   Charles Mathews's Riquet—not quite equal,
according to Planché, to Potier's original, which he had seen
in Paris—underwent a visible quick change, while Madame
Vestris's Princess Esmeralda burst out into gay and gracious
observations. The production, which wound up with a tableau
considered splendid at the time, caught on. It was the prelude
to twenty other fairy-extravaganzas of Planché's devising.
The reason why no modern adapter has chosen this otherwise
attractive subject to popular purpose may lie in the intense
difficulty of being ostentatiously brilliant—as Riquet has to be,

to atone for his unprepossessing looks—and at the same time of capturing the sympathies of the audience. We have not had many dramatists since Oscar Wilde who could accept this particular task with confidence.

Though it was Planché who started the habit of making the heroic verse a vehicle for puns, his comparatively mild efforts in this direction were soon outdone by his successors. Robert Reece was an especial expert in this tempting but, in the end, dangerous game of word-play. Excellent, like so many other ornaments, in the hands of a master, it soon becomes a boring obsession with smaller minds. To Shakespeare puns came so easily that he used them instinctively just as grace-notes on serious occasions, without any humorous intention at all; as when Lady Macbeth says—

> I'll gild the faces of the grooms withal,
> That it may seem their guilt.

In the Victorian burlesques, what began as a light-hearted quip ended by becoming a laborious infliction. Even Robert Reece's worst derangements were nothing to the atrocities of H. J. Byron and Burnand. Here are just a trio, taken at random—

> Fine horses those! That leader came from Sestos,
> Stands *fire* well, and so he counts *as best 'os*.

> A couch that's made 'midst buttercups he's shy on;
> The verdant sward how could a *dandy lie on*?

> You jeer at Pallas 'cos she's strict and staid;
> With all your railing you'll need *Pallas' aid*.

Pantomime

One would have thought that more than fifty years of this kind of thing would have been enough, considering that the heroic for serious purposes lasted only fifteen. Not at all! The time was to come for burlesque and fairy extravaganza to be exiled from the year-round theatre. But, long before then, they had been transferred—heroic verse, puns, and all— to that strange but ever-delightful gallimaufry of traditions— the modern English pantomime. There even the verse, though somewhat battered, bids fair to outlive the harlequinade— that last relic of the old Italian *commedia*. Whoever else talks prose, the Demon King and the Fairy Queen remain true to the heroic and even to the pun. Some people affect to shed rather pedantic tears over the dwindling to a shout and shower of crackers of the once prolonged exploits of Harlequin and Columbine, Clown and Pantaloon—not to mention the red-hot poker, the string of sausages, and the baffled policeman, lingering from the days when Sir Robert Peel's replacing of the old watchman was unpopular. But what is the use of keeping the outward shell when the spirit has gone? There can be no life without change.

The history of pantomime has now been repeated so often that there is no need to revert to it at large here. Goldoni tells us how the "impromptu" comedy of Italy, pillaged by Shakespeare and Molière, became in itself and in its own country stale and wearisome, though Gozzi did his best to bring it back to life. We know how Rich of Covent Garden—our own harlequin of genius—turned it into a dumb-show mime with dazzling success. We know how Grimaldi, to whom I shall be referring again later, created a new tradition for clown. But, when the original "Joey" was no more, his hoarse guffaw, painted, slashed cheeks, and wedge-tufted hair again grew meaningless and tedious, as a ritual and make-up handed down to dull-witted automatons.

Deburau

We know how, meanwhile, Deburau, the once forlorn and wandering child-acrobat of Napoleon's army, tramped and starved through almost every country in Europe. Then he came to the little Funambules, the "Tight-Rope Theatre," in Paris, and there created the entirely different clown that we have grown to love as Pierrot. I myself happen to have paid tribute to Deburau in my book, *The Story of Pierrot*—

> The night is darkest before the dawn. . . . Deburau was sitting in a neighbouring café—the Café de L'ours—preparatory, so the story goes, to throwing himself into the Seine. As he sat there, he overheard a little group of out-at-heel young actors and scribblers in high argument upon the art of the theatre. They talked of Talma, of tragedy, of comedy, of genius, of the spell of passion. Deburau listened. Out of the ashes of his despair a new hope, a new determination rose and glowed within his soul. He

also would be an actor! He would be tragedian, comedian—he, poor, despised Deburau, hissed from the stage where even dogs had won a cheer! He would bring into his lowly labours the soul that had tried in vain to express itself upon the tight-rope and balanced ladder! This grinning, clumsy lout of a pierrot he would make into a human character, touching the heart to tears as well as laughter. He would put his own sorrows into Pierrot, his own bitterness sweetened with sympathy. And they should laugh, too; yes, they should laugh! But it should be on Pierrot's side now—*with* him, not *at* him.

As it happened the little "Tight-Rope Theatre" was just at that time exactly ripe for Deburau's decision. . . . Short, dumb-show pantomime had been stealthily introduced, unwillingly and on sufferance, as a sort of framework for feats of agility. . . . With them grew the new Pierrot. Discarding the old grin and horse-play, Deburau made him a natural, gentle half-pathetic, half-humorous, wholly human figure, pale and cadaverous, with a smile of silent raillery for ever flickering round his lips. It had its instant result upon the fortunes of the Funambules. Pierrot became the rage of Paris. Poets, critics, playwrights, artists, flocked to the tiny twopenny pit.

Through it all Deburau won the glory that he deserved. Despite his triumphs, his wordly fortunes remained blighted by poverty, sickness and managerial tyranny. When all Paris was crowding to see him, he was giving six performances a day for thirty-five francs a week! His "dressing-room"—in reality a sort of earth-pit that had been dug out in making the foundations of the little theatre—continued to afford a favourably moist soil not only for mushrooms but for rheumatism and other ills. But his glory none could take from him. He was artist, creator. He—poor melancholy buffoon, who could not win a smile upon the tight-rope—was among the immortals!

National Inventions

Thus each nation to which the old Italian troupe wandered has made out of them the pantomime it deserved. Our own English pantomime—like our own English plum-pudding—has probably a more satisfying and varied set of ingredients than any. It is true that the spectacular "introduction" was introduced in the eighteenth century by Rich himself. The music-hall element, which came towards the end of the nineteenth, went far to swamping everything else for a while. But it would be difficult to gauge how much its still-abiding popularity owes to the burlesques and extravaganzas of Planché and his comrades—many of whose creations were, it may be mentioned, produced at Christmas time.

It owes to them much besides the verse and the puns that still haunt the memory of young and old pantomime-goers. It owes partly to them the feminine "boys," of whom Madame Vestris was an admired example, and the actual treatment of many of the stories. H. J. Byron's burlesque of Rossini's opera is the basis of practically all present Cinderella pantomimes, with its development of Dandini—or, as the name used to be, Dandino. Byron was also the inventor of "the Widow Twankey," who has been for so long indispensable to every *Aladdin* pantomime. This sore-tried lady made her first appearance— at any rate under that name—in the burlesque, *Aladdin, or The Wonderful Scamp*, presented at the old Strand Theatre. She was played by James Rogers to the Aladdin of Marie Wilton, the future Lady Bancroft. Lady Bancroft said of Rogers in her autobiography—

> There was no attempt to exaggerate in either dress or acting. When he entered, with a woe-begone face, and looked at the audience, nothing else was seen or heard for some seconds. But, however much Jimmy might provoke the audience to laughter, he would not be tempted to laugh himself.

New Stories

Doubtless the time will come—as it has already with *Peter Pan, Alice in Wonderland, Bluebell, Where the Rainbow Ends*, and other children's plays—when new stories will challenge *Cinderella, Aladdin, Dick Whittington, The Babes in the Wood*, and the rest of the old favourites. But the new stories are only the old ones with a difference. From whatever part of the world they come, one finds that they soon grow to be of the English pantomime-pattern—alike in character and purpose. They take upon themselves its simple Christmas idealism of youth and faith and love triumphant, of good overcoming evil, and of beauty revealed in and round a human world of homely jollity and struggle and humour. Probably the solar myth is at the bottom of it all. As in the days of the Roman Saturnalia, the turning of the sun is a signal for general topsy-turveydom. The exchange of sex is part of this; but our old friend, Phoebus

Apollo, is the last, as he was the first, principal boy. He gives this annual assurance to rows of glowing faces that, though the dark days are here, summer is on the way.

Also, the more pantomime changes—and it is always changing—the more it remains the same thing. In this it is like its own transformation scenes. We bid good-bye to Columbine; but who else is Cinderella? The rough-and-tumble comedy which used to enliven the harlequinade can happen just as easily in the Widow Twankey's kitchen or Dame Durden's school. Whatever happens, the fact is unchallengeable that the Christmas pantomime in England is more popular now than it has ever been. In its art it remains, and will probably remain for long still, a festival-medley of almost all that has gone to the making of our imaginative theatre. Here are, and will be, tragedy, comedy, farce, melodrama, ballet, song, spectacle, burlesque, and extravaganza. There is no use in saying that it ought to be this or that. It must be everything.

CHAPTER X

THE PROFESSION OF CRITICISM

NOW, what of criticism as a profession—its history and its practice? Between Kean and Irving, in England at any rate, it remained almost entirely dependent, for anything that could be called inspiration, upon the actor. As great acting itself was scarce, it followed that in these circumstances great criticism was scarcer still. Hardly a line lives on its own account. A host of biographies teem with theatrical anecdotes and descriptions of rowdy scenes in dingy playhouses, described by Sir Walter Scott as unfit for the presence of a decent woman. The "flashes of lightning" by which Shakespeare was read in Kean's earlier and soberer performances gleamed all the more memorably through the intervening darkness.

There was always Macready; but, in spite of efforts to grade him more highly, he relapses into a respected, intelligent, cultured, and temperamental actor-manager, who consistently pursued high ideals both of art and of life in a baffling time. No critic has commanded the passionate homage of the world for anything he wrote about Macready's acting, though Lewes's account of the farewell banquet is a good bit of sentimental reporting. One suspects that Macready was more interesting as a man than as an actor. William Archer's painstaking critical book about his career has not a tithe of the appeal of Macready's own autobiography. Sir Theodore Martin's monograph ends appropriately upon an "invitation to dinner" at which "were several distinguished men of letters, to meet whom was a great satisfaction." As Helen Faucit's husband, Sir Theodore should have discovered the immortal part if it had been there! But, whatever he was not, Macready was a great missionary. He faced fierce adventures in America. He took Shakespeare to Paris in 1827, and inspired Alexandre Dumas *Père* to the beginning of the romantic movement. He was a noble soul. Through all his conflicts he always, when at home, presided over family prayers—an example not, one fears, universally followed among actor-managers.

Grimaldi

One actor of unmistakable genius there was of that period; but of him we have curiously little critical record. Grimaldi would have lived and died like any other clown, had not the public made him their own. So the autobiography to the editing of which Charles Dickens lent—or, rather, sold—his name had to be published. It was given life by George Cruikshank's drawings. So far as Dickens is concerned he shows no sign of ever having seen Grimaldi. He devotes almost his entire preface to remembrances of having been to a pantomime in Richardson's Show as a child. The regular critics are hardly any better. Leigh Hunt and Planché write pretty stuff about Harlequin and Columbine. They took poor Joey for granted. For the rest, "we laughed ourselves hoarse," or "we lived our childhood over again," is considered good enough. Of Grimaldi's evidently remarkable performance in the tragic part of Orson in *Valentine and Orson* we can only guess between the lines of Dickens's *Life*—

> The effect produced on the audience by his personation of this character was intense. . . . It was in Grimaldi's opinion the most difficult he ever had to play; the multitude of passions requiring to be portrayed and the rapid succession in which it was necessary to present them before the spectators involving an unusual share both of mental and physical exertion. . . . He would stagger off the stage into a small room behind the prompter's box, and there, sinking into an arm-chair, give full vent to the emotions which he found it impossible to suppress.

The dramatists of the period failed to find any critic to write about them inspiringly. Douglas Jerrold's *Black-Eyed Susan* and sparkling comedies had to make their own fame. Bulwer Lytton even now lives mainly in satire. The study of him given by M. Augustin Filon, the French critic, in his book upon *The English Stage*, has an attractive candour—

> Bulwer passed himself off as a *grand seigneur* and a genius. He was really but a clever man and a dandy, who exploited literature for his social advancement. He affected a lofty originality. . . .

When at last it was discovered that his sublimity was a spurious sublimity, that his history was false history, his "middle ages" bric-a-brac, his poetry mere rhetoric, his democracy a farce, his human heart a heart that had never beat in a man's breast, his books mere windy bladders—well, it was too late. The game had been played successfully and was over—the squireen of Knebworth, the self-styled descendant of the Vikings, had founded a family and hooked a peerage.

Passing of the Patent

Grossly unfair as much of this is, where it is true it is refreshing for the time and place. But it is always to be remembered in Lytton's favour that to him more than anyone else was due the great change that was to be the making of modern criticism in England, as also of modern English drama. This was the freeing of the theatres from the old patent monopoly by the Theatres Act of 1843. With twenty theatres arriving within a generation where there had been only three and some unsanctioned entertainments, dramatic criticism soon became very nearly, if not quite, a whole-time profession. Among other things, the freeing of the theatre made Samuel Phelps's productions of Shakespeare possible at Sadler's Wells, haunted by the young clerk from Old Broad Street who was to become Henry Irving, and also by a young civil servant, named Clement Scott.

Meanwhile, a much more vigorous state of affairs was in evidence in France. There the romantic revival, which followed Macready's visit with Shakespeare, was giving the pens of critics and of dramatists—and of several who were both at once—plenty of exercise. Alexandre Dumas *Père* and Alfred de Vigny, Victor Hugo and Alfred de Musset—they were at least worth battling for or against. In regard to Victor Hugo and the extent of his influence upon the future, A. B. Walkley has some illuminating things to say in his essay on "Modern English and French Drama"—

Victor Hugo's plays . . . belong to the old drama of rhetoric. Every one of them is based upon an antithesis—a king at odds with a bandit, a queen enamoured of a lackey, a court fool turned tragic protagonist—and antithesis is a figure of rhetoric. Rhetoric, the monologue of Charles Quint before the tomb of Charlemagne. Rhetoric, the *scène des portraits*. Rhetoric, the address of Ruy Blas to the ministers. That grotesque document, the preface to Cromwell, so far as it had any meaning whatever, meant a rhetorical dramaturgy. The author of *Hernani* was not the first of the modern dramatists; he was the last of the rhetoricians. So much was written about the excitement over the *première* of *Hernani*, to say nothing of Gautier's red waistcoat, that at least the public was fooled into believing there must be something in it.

In France

Despite the romantic hurly-burly, classicism was by no means done with, either at the *Comédie Française* or elsewhere. The tragic intensity of Rachel in Racine and Corneille stirred George Henry Lewes to some fine critical prose—

> Rachel was the panther of the stage; with a panther's terrible beauty and undulating grace she moved and stood, glared and sprang. There always seemed something not human about her. She seemed made of different clay from her fellows—beautiful but not lovable. Those who never saw Edmund Kean may form a very good conception of him if they have seen Rachel. She was very much as a woman what he was as a man. If he was a lion, she was a panther. Her range, like Kean's was very limited; but her expression was perfect within that range. Scorn, triumph, rage, lust and merciless malignity she could represent in symbols of irresistible power; but she had little tenderness, no womanly, caressing softness, no gaiety, no heartiness. She was so graceful and so powerful that her air of dignity was incomparable; but somehow you always felt in her presence an indefinable suggestion of latent wickedness. . . . The finest of her performances was Phèdre. Nothing I have ever seen surpassed this picture of a soul torn by the conflicts of incestuous passion and struggling conscience. The unutterable mournfulness of her look and tone as she recognized the guilt of her desires, yet felt herself so possessed by them that escape was impossible, are things never to be forgotten.

How little some of the English critics of the pre-Victorian period were in touch with what was happening outside the little round of Drury Lane, Covent Garden, and the Haymarket may be gathered from the fact that in 1831 Leigh Hunt criticized favourably an adaptation of Victor Hugo's *Hernani*, without knowing the name of the author or what was then regarded as the epoch-marking importance of the play in dramatic history. This was soon to be altered. For at least thirty years—both before and after the coming of Boucicault's Irish dramas and of T. W. Robertson, himself enormously indebted to French example—the London stage was to be almost completely swamped with adaptations and translations from the French, stolen often without scruple or acknowledgment. To be thoroughly at home with Scribe and Legouvé, Ohnet, Labiche, and Sardou was the one essential to a conscientious critic of the eighteen-forties and 'fifties—above all if, as generally happened, he was himself a hack-translator. It may be that the theatre took time to realize what its new-born freedom meant.

The new playhouses that were cropping up, like the Princess's —where Charles Kean was to honour Shakespeare during the 'fifties with his "archaeological" revivals—the Strand, the St. James's, and the Royalty needed ready material. A French play translated overnight served the turn. John Oxenford of *The Times* is said to have been reproved by Delane for the number of letters received about the theatre—"a matter of no interest to anybody." It was a poor time for critics. Who could wish to be engaged in writing non-committal notices of the dreary rubbish of Falconer and Fitzball, counting it a great thing to be able to spot the Parisian source of some nasty farce or gory melodrama of the moment?

Irving and Critics

One cannot claim that, when the revival did come with Robertson in the 'sixties and Irving in the 'seventies, the critics had done much towards it. Robertson himself had been a critic of sorts; but it is clear from the journalistic tone represented by the "Owls" in his play, *Society*, that he was not proud of this. Drink and interminable talk and the borrowing of shillings in Bohemian resorts were among the credentials outwardly observed. Nor did the critics of the time do anything in particular to help Irving until he had helped himself. The provincial papers watched his progress for the most part with kindly but candid interest. Nothing like a prophecy arrived till he had already made a hit in London as Rawdon Scudamore in *Hunted Down*. When the company went on tour in *Meg's Diversion*, *The Liverpool Daily Post*, to which Irving's friend, Sir Edward Russell, then on *The Morning Star*, was afterwards to return as editor, came out with this—

> Mr. Irving's representation was a strong confirmation of our opinion that he is one of the few great actors on the stage. Not that his performance had any greatness in it; but for the reason that he succeeded in making it as remarkable an assumption as the limited area created by the dramatist would allow. He seemed superior to his part, and it would be difficult to drive away the impression that there is no rôle superior to him.

It rather looks as though Sir Edward had sent along a hint from town. Just six months before, at the St. James's itself, George Henry Lewes, sitting with George Eliot, had said to her: "That young man will soon be at the head of the English stage"; and she had answered: "I think he is there already."

The avalanche of praise that came from forty-one London newspapers after Irving's triumph in *The Bells* did not, after all, bespeak much originality, courage, or creative power in anyone else but Irving. Afterwards, it was comparatively easy to discuss at length what all London was already talking about. As a matter of fact, the assembly of critical impressions does not give to posterity a very clear notion of Irving's Hamlet, which I did not see, as he stopped playing it in the 'eighties. According to Clement Scott it was a realization of Hazlitt's idea of a Hamlet who "thinks aloud." According to Sir Edward Russell in the five columns of what was surely the longest criticism ever printed in a daily paper, it was a Hamlet who "aggravated his own excitements." For me, taking for granted Irving's imaginative power, I find two conversational phrases more enlightening than anything I have read in print. They were used by two utterly different people. One was Bram Stoker, who told me that the great thing about Irving's Hamlet was not its intellectual quality, but "Passion, my boy, passion!" The other was Walkley, who said that what he chiefly recalled was the way Irving's Hamlet "nagged Ophelia." There must have been some profoundly individual treatment of Hamlet's disillusionment over Ophelia's character, to which Irving was able to give full force at first, but which afterwards grew stale and artificial. This may be one reason why he stopped playing Hamlet so early.

Certainly Irving did much to make dramatic criticism worth doing—his productions at the Lyceum were the first for a long while over which even the average critic was allowed to turn the column. Yet the critics as a body do not shine in relation to him. Scott slashed at his Richelieu quite unfairly and at enormous length. He said he expected a "great" performance, and found it picturesque and intelligent, but dull. To what extent the play, which is at best a trashy piece of trickery, may have been to blame he did not say. As he was only a young man of 28 at the time, it is possible that he did not know. The libel-action over the address "To a Fashionable Tragedian" published in *Fun* in 1875 was not only justified in court with apologies offered to Irving, but might have been taken up by the critics. With all their faults, they can hardly have been what the address describes them. It says—

> With the hireling portion of the Press at your command, you have induced the vulgar and unthinking to consider you a model of histrionic ability and the pioneer of an intellectual and cultured school of dramatic art. . . . Elevate the drama, forsooth! You have canonized the cut-throat, you have anointed the assassin. Be content with the ghostly train of butchers you have foisted on public attention and let your next venture, at least, be innocent of slaughter. If your performance of Othello be trumpeted to the four winds of heaven by the gang of time-serving reporters in your employ, you will increase the epidemic of wife-murder one hundred-fold and degrade the national drama a further degree towards the level of the Penny Dreadful.

The title of "The Fashionable Tragedian" was to be used two years later for an equally regrettable but less personal attack in which William Archer, of all people—then a young fellow of 21—was concerned as part-author. It was published when Irving was going on a tour of the principal provincial cities, and a stack of copies was sent to be sold in each town during the week of Irving's visit. It described him as "one of the worst actors that ever trod the British stage," his Hamlet as a "weakminded puppy," his Macbeth as a "Uriah Heep in chain-armour," his Othello as an "enfuriated Sepoy," and his Richard as a "cheap Mephistopheles."

It says an infinite deal for Irving's tolerance that he made no complaint whatever about this pamphlet. Archer told me that, although he had a good deal to do with Irving afterwards, Irving never allowed himself to appear conscious of this youthful indiscretion on the part of one who was to prove the most honourable and respected critic of his time. In the same way, Joseph Knight attacked Irving's Macbeth remorselessly in *The Athenaeum*, saying "his slow pronunciation and his indescribable elongation of syllables bring the whole, occasionally, near burlesque." Yet Irving remained to the end a staunch friend of that fine scholar, who, he knew, was quite incapable of being moved by malice. Indeed, it was Irving who was ultimately to take the chair at a farewell banquet given to Joseph Knight by actors and actresses on his retirement.

Of course, there was an immense deal of truth in all that was said about Irving's mannerisms. Sometimes he was quite unintelligible—and the chuckle and trailing gait were always there. But so was the greatness. The saintly dignity of his Becket, the arch-roguery of his Mephistopheles, the sublimated irony of his Shylock, the ghastly horror of his Mathias, of his Dubosc in *The Lyons Mail*, and of his death-scene in *Louis XI*, and the rich, crusted comedy of his Gregory Brewster in *Waterloo*—all these were products of the stage-nurtured imagination and indomitable will of the man himself. He made one feel the adventure of life by presenting the extremes of villainy and virtue and idealizing both with the power and charm of his personality, itself born of the same imagination and will. From a critical point of view, Irving's art was peculiarly valuable because it was a standing refutation of the very false adage that "all great acting is a return to nature." Irving's acting was never a return to nature. The imaginative mask was never cast off.

His social self was an acted creation just like the others. The rarely-revealed man behind was the Somerset boy who became a City clerk and had been a struggling provincial actor, playing the policeman in a pantomime, while those who were glad to be considered his equals were at the University or being dandled into a learned profession. Irving's "natural" language was the west-country speech—to which he would sometimes revert, but only among his most intimate cronies. At the same time Irving's imagination reached from Becket to Dubosc.

He was Becket and he was Dubosc—and Hamlet, Mephistopheles, and Gregory Brewster, and all the rest—and absolutely
sincere in each character. His own private affairs and idiosyn-
crasies may have been used—as every good actor uses every
idea or emotion or atom of nervous energy he can summon up—
in the creation of a part. To him nature was just a help or
hindrance to imagination. The attempt to distinguish between
"character-parts" and "straight parts" was flouted once and
for all at the old Lyceum. Irving was all his characters; but
none of them was he. Roguery seemed sometimes the most
sympathetic thing; but there was no trace of it about his Becket
until it came to the personal speech of thanks—with smile—at
the finish. And as Becket he died.

Clement Scott

With the establishment of Irving on his throne the old-
fashioned English dramatic critic, who for me will always be
typified by Clement Scott, was in the splendour of his power.
I began my London playgoing towards the end of the 'eighties
and can vouch for the genuine good that Scott did for the
box-office by writing in a vein of almost lyrical enthusiasm of
actors and actresses—and getting it into to-morrow morning's
paper. He could turn out his column-and-a-bit in an hour—
which, as I know from experience, takes some doing—and
could see that nothing pertinent was missed out. His was
always a "full-dress" notice. He dealt with the play act by act.
He told the story, and gave picturesque impressions of the
production as such. If he did not like the play, he slashed at
it with such fury as to make people want to see it all the more.
But he never sneered. He never turned out the tame, half-
hearted, tired, and hurried quarter of a column that has all too
often to do duty for dramatic criticism in these days of fierce
competition and early publishing, when every line after eleven
o'clock has to be fought for.

He never left one in any doubt as to whether he thought
the play worth going to or not; and he had the faculty of
finding all sorts of reasons—sometimes quite low down in the
cast—why the answer should be in the affirmative. Scott's
reward was abundant. The velvet-collared cape, the flower

in the buttonhole, the special box, Lord Burnham's private carriage, the homage of pit and gallery—all were there. The time was lenient to his deficiencies. The problem-play had not arrived. Pinero was turning from farces for Mrs. John Wood at the Court to charming a London of tinkling hansoms with *Sweet Lavender*. Even *The Profligate* was provided with an alternative ending for those who wanted just apple-blossoms.

Moreover, the theatre was rich. It had no rivals. Thanks to Irving and the Bancrofts, Gilbert-and-Sullivan opera, the Kendals and John Hare, Hawtrey and Tree, and others, a huge, new, educated public was being attracted. The price of stalls had gone up in the West End, and tours were royal progresses. The actor-managers were making—and some of them squandering—fortunes. Since the great adventure of Bernhardt and the *Comédie Française* company at the Gaiety in 1879, hardly a season passed without the now "divine" Sarah paying London a visit. Scott was not of a nature to discuss profoundly the psychology of *Phèdre*; but he could always veer off to glamour and the *voix d'or*. On the other hand he could revel in Sardou and Adelphi-and-Princess's melodrama, and all the farces between *Our Boys* and *Charley's Aunt*. He helped to the last to feed the sacred lamp of burlesque; and regularly every Christmas he not only informed but convinced us that Sir Augustus Harris had "surpassed himself" in the Drury Lane pantomime.

Ibsen

Then came the impact of Ibsen, the arrival of the new criticism with Archer, Walkley, Shaw, and Grein, and the beginning of the end of Scott's empire, which was to crumple up finally with that ill-timed interview in *Great Thoughts* upon the morality of the stage. At this distance of time it is inconceivable that any critic of Scott's experience should have written such arrant rubbish as he did about *Ghosts*, so gallantly presented by one critic, J. T. Grein, at the inspiration of another, William Archer, and still revived at frequent intervals with discreet approval. Here are just a few of Scott's phrases—

An open drain; a loathsome sore unbandaged; a dirty act done publicly; a lazar-house with all its doors and windows

open. . . . Candid foulness. . . . Kotzebue turned bestial
and cynical. . . . Offensive cynicism. . . . Ibsen's melancholy
and malodorous world. . . . Absolutely loathsome and fetid.
. . . Gross almost putrid indecorum.

This was bad enough as coming from a critic who made no
bones about incestuous classics and went into raptures over
salacious Palais-Royal farce; but it was crowned by his sage
conclusion—

> It might have been a tragedy had it been treated by a man of
> genius. Handled by an egotist and a bungler, it is only a deplor-
> ably dull play. There are ideas in *Ghosts* that would have inspired
> a tragic poet. They are vulgarized and debased by the suburban
> Ibsen. You want a Shakespeare, or a Byron, or a Browning to
> attack the subject-matter of *Ghosts* as it ought to be attacked.

"This critic's literary judgment," Mr. Archer slyly and cog-
ently adds in his introduction to his own edition of the play,
"may be measured by his bracketing Shakespeare, Byron and
Browning as master-dramatists!" My own feeling is that it
was not sheer stupidity on Clement Scott's part. I used to sit
next him pretty frequently when he was deposed to a mere
seat in the stalls, and I did not find him a stupid man. He was
just highly emotional, and "boiled at a low temperature."
He had found it did not pay a dramatic critic of those days to
go deep. Also he did rightly gauge the feelings of a very great
many of his Victorian colleagues and fellow-playgoers, whose
attitude was that you can treat vice attractively and set it to
music, but must on no account warn people of its evil effects.
It was the old antagonism—not here of the Puritan mind to the
theatre, but of the theatre to the Puritan mind.

Forty years on, when the Vicar of Buxton considered the
play "hardly one for a festival," the fiery Clement found at
least one sympathizer. The whole thing really meant that, in
spite of Queen Victoria and all she stood for, the theatre was
in some phases still the Temple of Venus in Clement Scott's
day. Any of the old Plautine naughtinesses could be allowed, so
long as they were laughed over; but not a word against the
goddess! As it happens, *Ghosts* was one of the London revivals
in the 1951 Festival of Britain, with an admirable performance
by Beatrix Lehmann as Mrs. Alving. This time the critical

point of view was noticeably different. So far as unpleasant-
ness is concerned we have grown so used to it that sex-problems
as charming themes are beginning to be regarded as just
tedious. Another play revived in London during the 1951
Festival—*Breach of Marriage* by Dan Sutherland, presented
at the Scala, but not achieving even a week's run—dealt with
artificial insemination! Over *Ghosts* the general consensus of
current critical opinion was simply that it does not happen
to be Ibsen's best play. This view was, it may be recalled,
anticipated by Archer himself in bringing out the first English
translation.

William Archer

By the 'nineties dramatic criticism in London had undoubtedly become something like a small profession, though it
still had to be eked out for the most part with other occupa-
tions. Scott made a good salary and lived in Woburn Square;
but Walkley had to work all day in the General Post Office.
Bendall, a future censor, was also in the Civil Service. Nisbet
of *The Times* was editor of one of the first halfpenny-papers,
The Morning, and was also writer of the philosophic "Handbook"
of the old *The Referee*; Spencer Wilkinson, leader-writer and
expert in military history, was representing *The Morning Post*
when I first joined the confraternity. He was soon to be
replaced by G. E. Morrison, who was a barrister, as was E. F.
Spence, afterwards K.C., of the *Westminster Gazette*. Grein
spent his days in Mincing Lane. Joseph Knight was editor of
Notes and Queries. Most of the others filled up with book-
reviewing and other newspaper-work.

Apart from Scott there was just one critic who, though called
to the Bar, and with abilities that could easily have brought
him a competence there, set himself from the first to be a dramatic critic and nothing else and to give dramatic criticism
professional dignity and distinction on its own account.
This was William Archer. It was undoubtedly his work, not
only for Ibsen but for the intelligent playgoer in general, that
attracted me to the theatre—and how many others! I used to
read his articles in *The World* and recognize that this new
movement in the theatre was something already proving worth

the devotion of a man of wide culture, insight, sincerity, and charm—something different from the barren party-politics of that day, which seemed to be the only journalistic alternative; a bright adventure, in happy contrast to the drab repressions of the *fin-de-siècle* Victorian world.

"The Green Goddess"

Afterwards I came to know Archer pretty well, and was always conscious of the sacrifice his faith in the theatre must have entailed to this able, strong-minded Scandinavian-Scot. It meant having to write about rattle-trap farces and musical comedies in which he took not the remotest interest. In some ways no man could be imagined less temperamentally suited to the work of dramatic criticism. But, behind all his gaunt denials, he had something of Ibsen's own passion for "the place of light and sound," and a whimsical humour of his own. Perhaps the Scandinavian strain in his blood answered for much. In the irony of things, the success of his melodrama, *The Green Goddess*, which outraged nearly all the rules he himself had laid down in his book on *Playmaking*, came too late to bring him the satisfaction it should. A remarkable thing is that he did not plan *The Green Goddess* as a melodrama, and was much annoyed at hearing it compared with Dion Bouci-cault's *Jessie Brown, or The Relief of Lucknow*. He looked upon it as a philosophical phantasy. The Rajah—so admirably played by George Arliss—was supposed to some extent to represent his own last word upon things in general. From dramatic criticism Archer can never have made much. He got £10 a week for his articles in *The World*, which was £2 more than Shaw was making on *The Saturday Review* and more than three times as much as some of us other critics were getting. But even so, what a pittance for a man of his capacity— the honoured leader of his calling and a master of the language and literature of at least four Continental countries, let alone his own!

Walkley

Walkley, as I have already noted, was in almost every respect the antithesis of Archer. The lighter the thought with Archer, the more laborious the process. His mind, compared with Walkley's, was like the old clock at the Royal College of Science, which has some business to go through before it strikes the hour. With Walkley the apt allusion—from Boswell or Pickwick, Balzac or Sainte-Beuve—came with ease and immediacy. He was much less recondite than his cleverness led most people to think. His chief skill was in the grace he could put into small compass. The longer Walkley's article, the more danger there was of his revealing that he was not bursting with any great message. Some of his little paragraphs as "Spec" in *The Star* were much finer gems than his later columns in *The Times*. He was a master of happy incidentals —of things like a visit of Sir Roger de Coverley to Stonecutter Street, done in the style of Steele, and a musical criticism he once wrote in place of Shaw, signed "Bono di Corsetto" by way of a skit on Shaw's regular signature, "Corno di Bassetto."

I always used to feel that Walkley could have lived very contentedly in the eighteenth century, but was prepared to accept anything else that the nineteenth or this could give. So far as the theatre was concerned, he was a confessed opportunist. He could never have been the big gun in a campaign, as Archer was over Ibsen. It was enough for him that Coquelin and Bernhardt, Duse and Réjane turned up in the course of a season. If nothing else offered he would go to a music-hall and be remarkably entertaining over that. He was exactly fitted for the theatre. He knew—and told—all its secrets without having to ask; but he never cared about it with Archer's profound passion. With him it was lucrative recreation. His real delights were reading and music—he was an excellent pianist. How he found time for it all, with his immensely important work at the Post Office, is not so much a mystery as just a miracle, like his classical prowess at Oxford on a mathematical scholarship!

Shaw as Critic

Though Shaw dazzled everybody—as he openly intended to do—with those two years of brilliance on *The Saturday Review*, he was not, we also know, moved to it by any love of dramatic criticism. He had already won fame but not fortune as a dramatist. Why *Arms and the Man* was not a commerical success from the first is one of those things "no fella can understand." There it was—a masterpiece of comedy, still in some ways his best and brightest play, full of colour and fresh character, and without anything in it that could offend the most virginal Victorian maid. It had an excellent reception, apart from the gallery-voice with which Shaw so sportingly agreed— "But what are we two against so many?" Yet there was nothing doing. It is pleasant to believe that if half so good a play were to turn up now its saga would be very different.

No wonder Shaw determined to make a new reputation at all costs, and let the world know of him by the time his next play came along! So *The Saturday Review* criticisms were launched and did their work. What joyous reading they are still, in every kind, from *Boiled Heroine* to *Dear Harp of My Country*! As part of the inspiring biography of one of our greatest national geniuses with the heart of Dickens and the wit of Molière, and as literature in themselves, they will assuredly live. Whether they did unmixed good to criticism as a profession is another matter. As infallible judgments it would be an insult to Shaw to take them too seriously. He told us often enough the real reason why he "went for" Shakespeare, as offering the biggest and most revered target. His reluctance to give Irving full credit for that magnificent performance as Gregory Brewster needed no explanation, after all the other things he had written about Irving. Speaking personally, I was, and still remain, prepared to forgive Shaw anything he liked to say or do, whether as critic or as dramatist or as writer of "costume-debates." But not the next man—and that is the trouble. The success of Shaw's escapade as a dramatic critic has undoubtedly encouraged smaller people, without his qualifications or excuse, to get notoriety by reckless abuse.

J. T. Grein

Again in complete contrast was J. T. Grein, founder of the Independent Theatre, and the actual presenter not only of *Ghosts* but of Shaw's first play—or, rather, the play that Shaw and Archer wrote together—*Widowers' Houses*. Though not easily rivalled where a flair for acting, an all-embracing knowledge of the European drama, and a faculty for sustained hyperbole were concerned, Grein was at his greatest as a critic in deeds rather than words. Mr. Conal O'Riordan has put it very well in his foreword to "Michael Orme's" biography of her indomitable husband—

> He came as a simple man who did things, into a crowd of subtle men who talked and scribbled, and scribbled and talked, without producing any effect whatever except more talk and more scribbling. He ended by hearing Shaw say, and say truly, that he had changed the whole nature of the British theatre and changed it for the better. It has been born again in his hands.

Only those who, like myself, came into practical touch with Grein's spirit of buoyant and tireless enthusiasm for anything that could help the theatre or his fellow-critics can realize what a loss his death meant to both. His readiness, his eagerness, his friendliness, his unquenchable optimism, and sheer joy in any genuine endeavour for the good of art and of humanity—these have not left even a far-off likeness. He was not always wise, and he suffered tragically for some of his mistakes. But his resilience and the *panache* that he never lost were triumphant.

In my association with him over the founding of the Critics' Circle I soon came to recognize his pluck and initiative and complete unselfishness; and his personal charm and gaiety were a perpetual refreshment. His command of half a dozen languages—I remember his taking up Spanish late in life just by way of keeping his mind in trim—was of untold value. He was the only London critic who could respond adequately to Cavaliero Grasso in Grasso's own language, when we critics gave the Sicilian Players a supper, and that fine actor wanted, to our consternation, to kiss us all! In Canada, Grein's visit two years before his death to judge in the contest of amateur clubs at Lord Bessborough's invitation was a major event in the theatrical history of the Dominion. When it was discovered that he could talk French just as fluently as English, if not more so, the joy of the French-Canadians knew no bounds. It is to be doubted if any critic who ever lived faced worse odds than J. T. Grein, or fought a braver fight against undeserved opprobrium, or was, in the end, more universally and rightly beloved.

Pioneer Critics

These four men were the pioneers of modern dramatic criticism in England. Their friendship was for me a privilege worth many sacrifices. They all of them extended to me as a young man kindnesses and expressions of comradeship which amaze me all the more as the years go by, and the "hungry generations" succeed each other.

What of the present—and the future? From the professional standpoint, one must confess, dramatic criticism is not even what it was. The number of London daily and evening papers has dwindled from eighteen to fourteen. Even in those that are left, dramatic criticism is accorded on an average less than a quarter of the space it used to claim. As Bernard Shaw avowed in that talk of over fifty years ago, dramatic criticism does not pay on anything like a professional scale. Of the daily-and-evening critics certainly not more than six receive— even with film criticism added to that of the flesh-and-blood theatre—more than the salary of a suburban or provincial bank-manager. The minimum weekly-paper payment is beneath the trade-union wage of an agricultural labourer.

In these circumstances it is not surprising that nearly every dramatic critic has other irons in the fire. My old colleague, St. John Ervine—whose friendly tribute to me at a certain "testimonial dinner" I shall not forget—must have made far more out of his plays than out of all the criticisms and articles he has written. James Agate, who also did me a much-appreciated honour on the same occasion, distributed his "ego" to the world of books as well as to that of the theatre. He, too, wrote plays. Charles Morgan forsook criticism to be a successful novelist. Others have written novels, not with such outstanding results or without mentioning plays. Sydney W. Carroll, as a manager, has been responsible for some of the most memorable and beautiful productions of our time. Ashley Dukes became both dramatist and manager. In each capacity —with his own *The Man With a Load of Mischief* and T. S. Eliot's *Murder in the Cathedral*—he put us for ever in his debt.

In spite of its small emoluments, dramatic criticism has a far larger sphere of interest than it had when I started as critic for the long-vanished *The Morning Leader* in the year of

Queen Victoria's Diamond Jubilee. All sorts of new territories have been added. Apart from Ibsen and Sudermann, the sources of new creation were fifty years ago almost limited to London and Paris. Duse had for a long while to appear in Bernhardt parts utterly unsuited to her, making a good angel of Fédora and a saint of Marguerite Gautier. Afterwards she was to lend Italian souls for change to those thorough northerners, Magda and Hedda Gabler. True, there were some lovely reversions to native character in D'Annunzio's *La Gioconda* and *Francesca da Rimini* and Goldoni's *La Locandiera*.

Coquelin burst upon us with *Cyrano de Bergerac*. "Same old circus!"—such was Walkley's comment as my next door neighbour on that first night at the old Lyceum. But Rostand was a reaction—or, should one say, a flowering from the old stem of romantic rhetoric. America was sending over old-homestead melodrama of the *Alabama* type, and putting a new vigour into musical comedy with *The Belle of New York*. On the other hand it was giving us nothing to compare with Eugene O'Neill, Maxwell Anderson, Elmer Rice, George Kaufman, or Marc Connelly. Thanks to Grein we had some memorable seasons of German plays, with Hans Andersen and Else Gademann doing everything possible to win our hearts for Hauptmann. Somehow we never took to Gerhart—nor he to us. To the surprise of everybody, some critics included, it was the unabashed sentiment of Foerster's *Alt Heidelberg* that caught the favour of the British public—and then only when George Alexander snapped it up.

How infinitely larger a horizon opens out before the present-day critic and the present-day playgoer! It is true that Germany and Italy do not happen for the moment to be prolific of new and acceptable ideas in drama. Pirandello has come and gone. But a world of play-craft and stage-craft hitherto ignored has been revealed in the Russian plays—not only Chekhov but Gogol and Tolstoi and Dostoievsky, and a whole dramatic literature. Constantin Stanislavski's last admirable book, *The Actor Prepares*, has still much to teach us of the psychological intimacy aimed at and achieved by the Moscow Art Theatre. Whether the Soviet mass-theatres will prove equally fruitful remains to be seen. I rather doubt it. A new spirit is stirring in Oriental drama. Tagore's plays expressed very beautifully some not unchanging phases of Indian thought and emotion. Among his disciples time must find a successor. Both in China and Japan signs have not been wanting, when other activities have made it possible, of the arrival of modern drama welded of old romantic traditions and new social ideals.

America has become theatre-conscious—more, perhaps, than Hollywood approves. One could not ignore the activity in forty cities throughout the United States of the Federal Theatre movement, subsidized by the Government in the late 'thirties under the management of Hallie Flanagan. It is a pity its work, with expressionistic-industry plays and a "Living Newspaper," has now ceased. This type of drama may not be so formidable a rival to more deeply-imagined creation as some think. Possibly the organization was too hurried. But it all meant new life, new interest, and new material for criticism.

British Outlook

Throughout Great Britain itself the critical outlook is, at least, more inspiring than it was in my early days, when the touring of London successes and London actor-managers was almost as monotonous a purse-filling routine as the present-day exploitation of a film. The very struggles of the provincial theatre make helpful criticism all the more valuable. Every town with a repertory theatre—and there is a still growing number of them—is a possible centre for genuine creative work. It is by no means always a paying proposition; but it is none the less worth doing for that. Lessing got the equivalent of £120 a year as critic-in-ordinary to the Hamburg theatre, and the venture was a failure. But his *Hamburg Dramaturgy* is still a classic. No one was out to make much money over the founding of Dublin's Abbey Theatre, which was to give us an unrivalled procession of genius, from Yeats and Synge and Lady Gregory to Sean O'Casey.

In a good many of our provincial cities it does undoubtedly break one's heart to see how the individuality is going. To each there is nowadays a veneer of sameness—the same chromium-plated fronts of the same multiple-shops, the inevitable mammoth cinemas all showing the same films, the same

lights on the same motor-roads. All that seem to be left even
of some of our most endeared county-towns are a few tumble-
down houses in back-streets, a cathedral or parish-church,
and the old Theatre Royal, used sometimes as a second-class
film-house. But I believe this is only superficial. I believe
that underneath there nearly always does exist a character and
humanity and home-love which demand something more than
mechanical mass-expression. Even there, in little halls and
upper-rooms, with companies of amateurs or valiant young
professionals working like demons for next to nothing, the
living drama is being born again.

We can learn much from the histories of the Liverpool
Playhouse, of the Norwich Maddermarket, and of repertory
enterprises like those at Birmingham, York, Coventry, and
Bristol. They serve to show what can be done when high purpose and sincere enthusiasm and wise conduct combine. The
immense growth of the amateur movement is another proof
that the art of the theatre is a natural outcrop of the human
spirit. Everywhere the dramatist, actor, and critic has each
his work to do in fostering the three essentials—play, performance, and audience. In the West End, with its forty theatres
serving an eight-million population, the labours of the dwindled
company of dramatic critics are far more arduous than they
were. Instead of writing at leisure long notices of two or three
new plays a week, they have to write, or telephone, five or
six short ones in far more trying circumstances. Here, too, is
a labour only occasionally rewarded with the arrival of a play
that it is an unmixed delight to see and praise. On the whole,
one must confess, the commercial managers as a body do keep
the theatre of intelligence going in the face sometimes of stagger-
ing losses. Thanks to them, the spoken drama has survived
the challenge of ballet and spectacle, both on and off the ice,
as it did that of the film and broadcasting.

National Theatre

At the same time I certainly feel that criticism would
benefit by some such artistic basis as should be afforded by
the National Theatre, of which the foundation stone has already
been royally laid at the Shot-Tower site on the Surrey bank

of the Thames. To this £1,000,000 has already been voted by Parliament—not nearly enough, of course, for the building of the two theatres, large and small, that will be necessary, and for the endowment of the elaborate organization that will have to go with them. We are told that it will be several years yet before we shall see the promised structure on the Thames-bank, let alone the other essentials. But everything must have a beginning sometime. The sooner we start the better!

I conceive the National Threate, like the *Comédie Française*, not only as an august home of tradition, but as a nursery of new ideas and new hopes for the classics of the future. In either direction it will supply a critical standard. In the present rough-and-tumble circumstances, the wonder is that English journalism should have produced so many good critics. Even in the days of Sarcey and Lemaître no one suggested that the critical corps of Paris outshone the more haphazard assemblage of the London theatres. But I believe strongly that a repertory theatre in London of the highest class, with something of an official sanction and support, would give the drama—and criticism with it—a dignity and standing that both have lacked. All through my critical career I have been oppressed with the assumption—a true one, doubtless, from a commercial point of view—that the theatre is just a place of entertainment. I have been told that, for newspaper purposes, I must judge plays primarily, if not solely, by their "entertainment value." From this compulsion I am happy now to be free. I would not go so far, perhaps, as did my friend, the late Henry Arthur Jones, in his book, *The Foundations of National Drama*. He sets down there, as one of his "corner stones"—

> The severance of the drama from popular entertainment: the recognition of it as a fine art which, though its lowest ranges must always compound with mere popular entertainment, and be confused with it, is yet essentially something different, transcends it, and in its higher ranges is inmarked and eternal antagonism to popular entertainment.

Critical Standard

My own feeling is that the word "popular" is wrong in this connexion. I am sure that what the author of *The Silver King* really means is just weak concession to the stupid and the sensual. But this is by no means always "popular." The most degrading productions that I have seen have been exclusive and expensive luxury-shows for tired businessmen. In his main contention Jones was right enough. The establishment of a National Theatre would supply one theatre at any rate where plays would be criticized without fear or favour by the highest standard. Those criticisms would be far more worth reading than the extravagant praise given, for instance, to the sometimes not wholly satisfying productions at the Old Vic, as it stands now, with reservations that better was not to be expected at a "people's theatre."

One effect upon criticism that would, I think, result from the establishment of a National Theatre in London would be a closer approach between scholars and workaday critics. The *Comédie Française* has always afforded this link between the academic and the commercial theatre, which is good for both. In America the gap has been more happily spanned than here. Critics like Brooks Atkinson, George Jean Nathan, and John Mason Brown are nearer to the world of Brander Matthews and Professor Baker than most of Fleet Street is to that of Dr. Pollard or Sir Edmund Chambers. Also a National Theatre would help the education of younger critics in the right playing of Shakespeare and suggest the best and most faithful compromise in modern production. As it is, the temptation towards stunts on the part of ambitious and hurried producers anxious for notoriety tends to be encouraged by young critics, who cannot make comparisons with what they have not seen.

Whatever happens on the Surrey-side site, I must confess to hoping that something tributary to the theatre will be done with the earlier site in South Kensington, where Bernard Shaw engaged in a founding ceremony with a sod of earth some years ago. Although nominally "exchanged" for the present pitch, it could still be used by the L.C.C.; and it happens to be an admirable site for what might be called West-End purposes. It is just about half-way between two theatres to which we owe very much of the kind of work a National Theatre should do. One is the old Court Theatre, which gave us nearly all that was best in the drama of the first ten years of this century, and the other is the Lyric, Hammersmith, where Gay and Dryden were made to live again to happy if not permanent purpose. Both these theatres, to which the gratitude of every true lover of the drama who frequented them goes forth, have afforded— each in its own way—proof that there is a London public ready to respond to any fine work set upon the stage. During the years in which we shall be waiting for a more central and monumental fulfilment, I strongly believe that, with something like national backing, a body of well-purposed and energetic pioneers could set upon that site in South Kensington an ideal local centre and, for many purposes, an excellent critics' playhouse. While the national architecture is being evolved, here is a little spot which would serve as a repository for uncommercial drama and provide a stimulus to new endeavour.

CHAPTER XI

FROM PRESENT TO FUTURE

NOW that we have been through the drama of most of the ages from the critic's point of view, it may be useful to end with some suggestions for the future. For the time being I will confine myself to the daily paper. Criticism has changed there more than elsewhere. As we have seen, it now fills only a quarter of the space given it in my first days, and it has to be done much earlier. When, as I have already mentioned, I started over fifty years ago as dramatic critic of *The Morning Leader*, edited by Gordon Hewart, the future Lord Chief Justice—and what an understanding and blithe young editor he was! One could go on writing till half-past one in the morning. There was time to have some supper and collect one's thoughts before beginning—that is to say, if the performance ended at eleven. It was by no means rare then for a spectacular show to go on till half-past twelve or one o'clock, in which case these luxuries had to be forfeited.

Anyhow, the more one could write, the better everybody was pleased—except, on some occasions, the chief sub-editor. To be able to spin it out was the great thing. The world of news was nothing like as big as it is to-day. There was, in normal circumstances, any amount of space that needed filling, and dramatic criticism was good, cheap copy. So the more, the merrier! All this is, of course, completely altered now. In some cases, a short paragraph, telephoned after the first act and corrected for a later edition afterwards, if the prophecy has proved entirely wrong, passes for a considered judgment upon the play.

Negation of Criticism

In the matter of difficulty I do not think there is much to choose between the two. If it is well done and proves a true and fair impression of the play, as sometimes does happen, the telephoned paragraph is a good piece of journalistic anticipation.

For a certain number of plays, which can be seen to be of no use at all almost from the rise of the curtain, it is satisfactory enough to the public. They will be spared the disappointment of going to the theatre. But when the play is a really good one, or when it has good work which deserves appreciation and encouragement even in failure, or when a piece of fine acting emerges—then this kind of criticism is of little use. It is, at heart, just a negation of criticism, which entails the perception of good just as much as bad. It is a verdict without evidence, which is absurd.

In view of these and other matters, I have been interested in recalling some observations of my own, made nearly fifty years ago in *Journalism as a Profession*, edited by Arthur Lawrence—

> The first thing that the public want to know from a daily paper is whether a new play is worth going to or not. If it is, they want to know why it is worth going to. They want to get an idea of what sort of thing it is. They want to know of acting reputations lost or won. They also want "the story"—and that is where the really difficult part of daily-paper criticism comes in. It may be considered that this is a very humble view of dramatic criticism, offering the critic no distinction from a reporter of current events —of funerals and festivals, Parliamentary speeches and accidents on the Embankment. This is far from being the case. The incidents of a play are not events. They never happened. A mere report of them—which, if they had really happened, would be of enthralling interest—is the dullest of all dull reading.
>
> What is it, then, that has happened in a theatre? A certain number of people have gathered together and, by the various means that compose the art of the dramatist, the actor, the scene-painter and the musician, have been moved to the emotions of joy, hope, sorrow or mirth, and possibly have received at the same time some intellectual enlightenment. The dramatic critic has not only to state such occurrences, which is very easily done and takes a line or two. He must also show how it was done, for the public has a great faculty of disbelief. He must find out the various contributing elements to this triumph (or, perhaps, failure) of illusion.
>
> Of these the principal is probably—though by no means necessarily—"the story." But the real story of a play would occupy some three or four columns of a newspaper. The dramatic critic has to choose just such incidents as go to prove his case for or against the play, make them intelligible by coherence, lucid by

explanation, and interesting by atmosphere. He must, in effect, tell not the story of the play, but a parallel story of his own, true to the story of the play, but enormously concentrated and simplified in incident, and also very much altered in emphasis—for it is generally just those matters which seem most important and exciting on the stage which are least suggestive on paper.

He has by this story of his to convey in a few lines the emotions which it has taken the people behind the footlights three hours to produce. Having done this, he has to bring in, just in their right proportion, word-pictures of such acting and scenery as have contributed to the effect—pictures that must be more varied than need be any recountal of fact. All this he has to do in the space of an hour, or an hour and a half, with the exercise, if it is well done, of both analytical and imaginative qualities of the highest order. . . . So far from being the useless and surfeited monopolizer of a newspaper-office's complimentary pleasures, he is engaged in one of the most difficult and necessary tasks that the varied labours of daily journalism can afford.

Telling the Story

Needless as much of this would seem to be now, my memory tells me that the hour or hour and a half were employed in conscientious effort to fulfil a task which the present-day daily-paper critic simply does not worry about. The "story," which we of that time used to take such pains over, was an elaborate and much-prized little vignette, trying definitely to create a kind of illusion in the reader that he, like the critic, had seen the play. Sometimes one would go through the whole fable. When it was a pretty, well-rounded story, this served best. Sometimes, in highly dramatic pieces, one seized upon a particular scene, and contented oneself with what led up to it. But always the telling of the story in the criticism was intended as a work of art. It was valuable to the theatre because it attracted the public—sometimes to an indifferent play, but Theseus would have found pardon for that. It was pleasant reading to those who, for some reason or other, would not be likely to see the play at all.

I doubt if there is any kind of criticism now in which this old art of telling the story is practised. There simply is not room for it in the present daily-paper notices. Even the evening papers have to forfeit space for a photograph of the principal player or scene—not to mention fashion-studies of members of the audience—which means an instant death of illusion on the reader's part. The weekly critic has either to write round pictures or devote himself to some excursion in critical theory, on the assumption that his readers have either heard all about the play already or do not want to know. Some of them, like my old friend Agate, would on occasion openly deal with anything else but the play, helped by a book-shelf and a few random allusions.

First Essential

On the other hand the first practical essential of daily-paper dramatic criticism fifty years ago remains even more surely the first practical essential of daily-paper dramatic criticism to-day. It is to decide whether or not a play is worth going to. Although, in the conditions prevailing, present-day criticism is often extremely well done, it is a curious fact that this "A" of the critical alphabet is not always paid sufficient attention to. When there is an obvious, exciting, and brilliant success, the occurrence can hardly help being apparent. Even then, the temptation to be different—more insistent with the later weeklies—sometimes leads the critic to "hint a fault and hesi-tate dislike" on his own account. But when the play is not an unmistakable and outstanding winner—and I have seen many plays run for years that were half-heartedly received or even booed on their first night—it is remarkable how few critics can convey to their readers exactly what those readers want to know.

I have before me, as it happens, some current notices in daily papers about a play I do not chance to have seen. Not one of them gives me a clear notion whether, as a reader, I should find it worth while to pay for a seat. One critic says that it "may be a good play," but that it deals with a subject of which he is personally ignorant. Another recalls his emotions on seeing a real accident something like one in the play. Another confides to us that he first saw the leading lady when he was a boy at school. At the same time they all combine in confessing that it was well-acted, well-written, and favourably received. What is one to think? None of them attempts—or, indeed, could attempt in the space accorded—to "tell the story," with the help of which I might come to my own conclusion.

One is reminded of the tale told by John Oxenford, the celebrated former critic of *The Times*. He is said to have attended a new production at the now-vanished Olympic Theatre with a lady-friend, and was accorded a box, in which he went to sleep. Waking up with a start at the conclusion, he asked his companion to tell him all she could about it and her opinion of its merits, with a view to his notice in next morning's paper. "Well," she is recorded to have answered, "I should call it one of those what-d'you-take-me-for sort of plays." Nowadays, people are all too often led to believe that there is a plethora of plays of this description being presented.

Personality

Much of this self-centred attitude on the part of some present-day daily-paper critics is, of course, understandable and pardonable. Each one naturally feels the need of keeping his end up as a personality. It is a healthy ambition, though hardly helped by scraps of autobiography and self-analysis, unless these have something either remarkable or sympathetic about them. A free individual expression of opinion on the critic's part is all-important—a very different thing from indecisive self-assertion. The rule for playwrights laid down by Somerset Maugham—"Have something to say, and stick to the point"—might almost, if one believed in rules, be transferred to critics. But it all depends upon what the "something" is, and whether the "point" is in any way relevant to the play under consideration. The cult of personality at the expense of other critical duties is, of course, not a new thing, nor is it confined to this side of the Atlantic.

Though a believer that "criticism must be personal or nothing," George Jean Nathan writes in his book, *Criticism and Drama*—

> The trouble with dramatic criticism in America, speaking generally, is that where it is not frankly reportorial it too often seeks to exhibit a personality when there exists no personality to exhibit. Himself, perhaps, conscious of this lack, the critic indulges in heroic makeshifts to inject into his writings a note of individuality, and the only individuality that comes out of his perspirations is of a piece with the bearded lady or the dog-faced boy. The college-professor who, having nothing to say, tries to

give his criticism an august air by figuratively attaching to it a pair of whiskers and horn-glasses; the suburban college-professor who sedulously practises an aloofness from the madding crowd that his soul longs to be part of; the college-professor who postures as a man of the world; the newspaper-reporter who postures as a college-professor; the journalist who performs in terms of Art between the Saks and Gimbel advertisements—these and others like them are the sad comedians in the tragical crew. In their heavy attempts to live up to their fancy-dress costumes, in their laborious efforts to conceal their humdrum personalities in the uncomfortable gauds of Petruchio and Gobbo, they betray themselves even to the 'bus boys. The same performer cannot occupy the rôles of Polonius and Hamlet even in a tank-town troupe.

This is needlessly cruel, but it does emphasize what is an undoubtedly growing tendency—and one which is not only the critic's fault. The fact that all sorts of honest, workaday fellows are tempted to try to assert personalities regardless of the play about which they are supposed to be writing is due in some measure, as I have said, to smaller space and larger competition. It is also partly brought about by a public who are less and less trained to exercise thought and imagination. They respond to personal assertion because this is more easily understood than ideas with a less simple contour.

Impressionism

The old controversy, too, of impressionism as against information comes in. Nathan, as we have seen, throws passing scorn upon what he calls "frankly reportorial" or informative criticism. Was it a very wise taunt? There is no question that many young critics of the present time are so anxious not to be classed as reporters that they purposely avoid making any statement of impersonal fact at all—a very stupid and snobbish attitude. On these matters I find little reason to revise an opinion I set down recently in some articles on "Aspects of Criticism." They were contributed to *Theatre and Stage*, Harold Downs's invaluable compendium of present-day theatrical knowledge, to which I am indebted for several other remarks included in the present chapter—

To those who have practised criticism for any length of time there is a very plain answer to the long-vexed question as to whether it should be impressionistic or informative. It must be both. I have no patience with some current criticism which purports to be so exclusively impressionistic that it conveys no idea of what the play is about, whether or not it is worth seeing, of what kind the production is, or who appeared in it and in what characters. This is not criticism. It is just tomfoolery. It thrives only in circumstances definitely hostile to the theatre. . . .

At the same time, the older I grow, the more I find it advisable and possible to rely on my own subconscious impressions. I have found these to be always right, as against any argued or external representation to the contrary. I do not believe in thinking out my notice during the play as so many do. I believe in being an absolutely natural playgoer up to the fall of the curtain; then an absolutely unnatural journalist. With impressions collected, good journalism demands that one should be just as informative as time and space permit.

Critic-dramatist

A charge once made to me by the late James Welch concerning the critic-dramatists of an earlier generation would be, as we have already seen, to some extent true of the critics of the present time. It was at the first performance of an afterwards successful farce, *When Knights were Bold*. I happened to be seeing him about some other business in his dressing-room. The play was not going too well. He put this down to the apathetic demeanour of the critics present. "I know those ——critics," he said, shaking his fist in the direction of the auditorium, "disappointed dramatists, every man jack of them!"

Quite seriously the element of truth in this has to do with a personal problem to be earnestly considered by any writer entering upon a career in the theatre. Is criticism a good apprenticeship to playwriting? Is it worth while for a young man who wants to become a playwright to try to get into criticism with a view to getting out of it? My own experience is that when a successful dramatist has been also a successful critic things have nearly always happened the other way round. Shaw, Ervine, and Ashley Dukes were all dramatists before they were critics. Archer's ultimate success with *The Green Goddess* was largely due to the fact that he had been writing plays all his life. He had, indeed, tried his hand at them long before he decided to make criticism his major business. Walkley used to aver, with a twinkle of the eye, that he had "never written a play"; but he did not say that he had never tried.

So, too, with the practising critics of to-day. At the next Christmas revival of Harriet Jay's play, the shade of James Welch might still shake a ghostly fist from the other side of the curtain. The critics would probably be playing truant in an always busy week; but it would still be true that nearly every one of them has at some time or other toyed with the idea of becoming a dramatist himself. After all, it is only reasonable that this should be so. A successful play brings its author a fortune and good plays are scarce. James Welch himself, in spite of his candour, pleaded with me in vain to write a play for him in which he should be both comic and sympathetic. Criticism supplies at best an insignificant income compared with that of the social paragraphist who shares the first-night seats. A young man who loved the stage and did not try first for the richer prize would probably not be much good as a critic or as anything else.

There is no disgrace in having tried and failed. The disgrace would be in not having tried. How many brilliant and even great men have made the trial and not succeeded in being successful dramatists? When Mark Twain was urged to write a play his answer was: "Sir, I have written fifty." Dr. Johnson's effort with *Irene* did not prevent him from contending that, as a dramatic critic, he "knew more about mutton than any sheep." For those who have tried as dramatists and even partially succeeded, I myself do not think criticism—that is to say, the daily drudgery—is of much use. I have seen some well-equipped creative minds completely staled by it. Shaw tells us that his brief two years as *The Saturday Review* critic "nearly killed him." St. John Ervine and Ashley Dukes have very wisely given up regular first-night criticism. On the other hand there is such a thing as a born critic—that is to say, a born journalist with a love of, and instinct for, the theatre, untainted by personal vanity or disappointment, or idle delusions of any kind. For such a man—or woman, for there is no reason why Aphra Behn and Mrs. Inchbald should not have their successors in England as well as America—dramatic criticism, judiciously mixed with other avocations, remains even now worth the industry and sacrifices it entails. It can never, on its own account, lead to wealth; but it may conduce to happiness and even to honour.

Aspirants

Perhaps I should give here a few suggestions for those who, in spite of all warnings, are still intending critics. We will suppose that a boy is just leaving school and has made up his mind that he wants to be a dramatic critic for a daily paper. How is he to set about it? Shall he go to a university, or become immediately a journalistic apprentice, or enter the Civil Service, or try his luck on the stage, or in films, or in a broadcasting studio? Or should he forget all about it and pursue some calling that will take him for a discreet period into the heart of Africa or the back-blocks of Australia—anywhere where there is least likelihood of there being any theatre at all—and then rely upon an entirely fresh outlook? I have mentioned these various possibilities because I have known critics who have arrived by each road. They have succeeded or failed with curiously little regard to their past. Moreover, the number of now-practising critics who came to the theatre direct from one or other of the world-wars makes an analysis of precedent still more unreliable.

Speaking from a pretty large experience, I can say that I have found it best to advise all young men who contemplate taking up daily dramatic criticism as a profession to ask themselves what their real aim is. Do they really want to be critics? Or is not all they want just to have an opportunity for plenty of enjoyable playgoing and to meet the distinguished people who are recorded as going to first nights? If their wishes, tastes, and talents lie in any of these directions I would urge them to steer clear of criticism. All these ends are better obtainable by other means.

Actor-critic

The stage itself, for instance, needs no roundabout approach. There is nothing whatever to stop any boy or girl going direct to one of our dramatic schools and learning to become an actor or actress. The old days when he or she had to run away from home or plunge into provincial melodrama—excellent school as it was—are over now. As for the would-be dramatist, I have already tried to show that nearly all the critic-dramatists who have done well in the later capacity were dramatists first and critics afterwards. Even so, a spell on the stage itself, either as actor or producer, or any sort of activity in the social world, is a better preparation for dramaturgy than criticism. The experience to be got in helping to stage a round of classics with a struggling repertory company is likely to be more useful to a budding dramatist than anything he will learn in a news-paper-office. Newspaper-work will tend to make him—as it should—a critic instead. The most important thing for him, either way, is that there should be as many outlying adventures at home and abroad as he has pluck to enter upon.

Then there is the young man or young woman who just likes the theatre and thinks it would be jolly to go to exciting first nights free of charge. Here again every reason exists to dissuade any such young people from going into training for the profession of criticism. When it comes to going every night, year after year, to the same recurring theatres, meeting the same sort of people at the same sort of plays, and seeing the same players acting in one very much as they did in another, the glamour soon disappears unless there is a very much deeper love of the theatre than attendance at first nights answers for. To aspirants of this type my advice is that they should go into some much more lucrative profession. The more money they make, the more plays they will be able to go to, and the more they will enjoy them by spending their time in something quite different during the day.

"Born Critic"

I can now come to that curiously rare bird—the "born critic" I have mentioned—the man, woman, boy, or girl, whose talent is for journalism and who has at the same time a pro-found love of the theatre. My own feeling is that for the young would-be critic of this description the best training is to take the playgoing for granted and begin with general newspaper-work. The all-round journalist who is, and is known to be, keen about the theatre will get his opportunity long before the exclusively theatrical student. He will also be more likely to make good with it than the man who has still to acquire a sense of proportional values and other instinctive promptings which come naturally to the trained mind and hand.

The difference between the competent daily-paper critic and the amateur is not, after all, that he goes to theatres and sees plays. Everybody does that. It is that he is able to turn out on the spot—or at a newspaper-office immediately afterwards—a clear, bright, accurate assessment, which has an interest and character and entertainment-value of its own and is something that everyone will want to read. It is the power of being at once lively and judicious and of being so at break-neck speed, with every paragraph and sentence formulated, as it comes, to an exact number of words. This rapid blending of character and truth, the seizing of salient points, and the exercise of imagination capable of conveying ideas into immediate print cannot be managed without experience. I myself went through the provincial "mill," and owe an incalculable deal to it. I had done practically everything on the editorial side of newspapers both in town and country, from junior reporter to editor, before I was given, at 22 years of age, my first appointment as dramatic critic for a London daily. It was on the strength of a notice of the first performance of Forbes-Robertson's Hamlet at the Lyceum—on 11th September, 1897—written from the third row standing behind the gallery.

Universities

Granted wide reading and ardent playgoing—without which there would be no hope for him at all—I do not think the intending critic who takes the trouble to be a journalist need fear missing a few seasons of specialized theatrical knowledge. This will come soon enough. I can assure him that after twenty or thirty years he will find he knows, if anything, too much. To keep young of heart and in sympathy with the supposed new movements which are always cropping up he will have to be constantly deciding what it is best to pretend to have forgotten.

I am often asked whether a university training is good for an intending critic. Of course, it is. It is so particularly just now, when not only Oxford and Cambridge, but London

University and others, are paying a remarkable amount of attention to the theatre, both officially and otherwise. The London University diploma has an especial value. But I do not believe in specializing too early. The groundwork, classical and modern, must be broad and thorough. All the lectures on dramatic theory—inspiring though they may sometimes be—will not replace sound scholarship and the mastery of at least three languages. Meanwhile to be in the swim of the theatre "groups" is a great thing. The Oxford University Dramatic Society—more familiar to us all as the O.U.D.S.—the Cambridge A.D.C., and kindred amateur clubs at other universities have borne notable fruit among critics as well as among actors and dramatists. This will, I think, happen still more. It is to be remembered, however, that journalism has to be learned afterwards just the same, with or without a degree. This is the shock in store. The undergraduate essay suffers all too frequently from a parade of borrowed views, an assumption of unpossessed knowledge, a fear of expressing sincere and simple-hearted enthusiasm, and other characteristics referred to by Longinus as "puerile." These make it sometimes an exact example of how dramatic criticism should not be written.

Specializing

We will assume now that our young friend has been to a university, has had some drilling in journalism, and has gone about the world just as much as his pocket and temperament have made possible. If he is known as a playgoer it will not be long before he is given his trial as a "second-string" critic. Presuming that he is successful, he will have to decide how far to specialize and how far not. This is an extremely important point. It is one already settled for civil servants, barristers, and others with unjournalistic day-time work—though they have troubles of their own. A barrister's legal duties may be graded down to none at all, if he wishes; but the Civil Service is more exacting than it was, and dramatic criticism in London, with first performances almost every night instead of two or three times a week, is growing a little too arduous to be looked upon as a mere hobby.

Accordingly the young journalist who is beginning his career

will soon have to choose what else he is going to do. Probably
he will already have sacrificed, for dramatic criticism, much
more profitable and promising chances in political work,
foreign correspondence, and other of the countless paths that
may lead to great things in and from the "street of adventure."
He has chosen a branch of journalism which will soon cease to
be an adventure at all, and will certainly be less so when he is
60 than when he is 23 years of age. Granted a full understanding
and acceptance of this state of affairs, what is the best kind of
other work to be doing? I must again set it down as a fact
which cannot be too strongly emphasized for the young journalist that almost without exception dramatic criticism, even
on the leading national newspapers, has to be reinforced by other
employment, journalistic or no. The few apparent exceptions
are mostly critics who also deal with theatrical "news," or
cover films as well, or write criticism for a number of papers.

Press Agent

I myself have tried all these alternatives, each of them for
many years, and none is satisfactory. Theatrical news-gathering
has its value for a young critic. I myself owe some priceless
friendships to it, and it gives a knowledge of what may be
called stage politics that the isolated student sometimes misses.
To any critic, however, who has arrived at a position in which his
opinion counts, the difficulty of being a judge by night and a
news-hunter by both day and night as well is a constant hindrance
in either direction. This side of newpaper-work has also been
very much complicated—or perhaps I should say simplified—
since the beginning of my critical career by the arrival of the
press agent—or theatre representative, as he now prefers to call
himself. He—or she, for the number of ladies in a business where
charm naturally counts for much has been growing fast—was
introduced from America shortly after the turn of the century,
and has become an extremely important factor in theatre-life.

The pioneer on our side of the Atlantic was the late Louis
Nethersole. The late Sir Charles Cochran came close upon
him, but always admitted Nethersole's priority. Louis had
been taking his sister, Olga, round America, and set himself
up as London's first liaison officer between newspapers and

the management, representing Lee Shubert over the Sothern and the Marlowe season at the Waldorf in 1907. He was soon followed by others, till the practice of each theatre or production having a special purveyor of paragraphs and photographs and news-ideas became general. The Press agent nowadays not only sends out news, but acts as host at journalistic receptions, and sees to the personal publicity of stars, and others. I have known of cases in which nearly every member of a company has had a different Press agent to supplement the attentions of the staff officials employed by the management. In such matters the recent establishment of an Association of Theatre Representatives has proved distinctly useful.

Conversational

There was nothing of this when I started. Many editors objected to putting in announcements of coming productions anywhere else but "under the clock" and at customary rates. Those papers that did indulge in a column of theatrical talk were accommodated in this respect by the critic himself, who went and saw the actual managers. I had a regular day each week for visiting Tree, Alexander, and George Edwardes, and saw others as occasion served. These conversations were by no means confined to news. They were more or less friendly conferences in which one learned an enormous deal of the other side—especially as the barrier between the stage and the outer world was much more marked then, than it is now. Possibly the manager himself was sometimes given a fresh point of view. But always, sooner or later, the time came when one's duty as a critic had to be candidly done, and a cold spell set in.

On the whole, I think Press agents have been a benefit— indeed they have become necessary with the present enlargement of the personal and photographic element in news. Being concerned with journalists all their time, they understand difficulties a good deal better than the old-world manager used to, and they have taken over work a critic could never do. I might add that Press agency is a calling that may well be thought of by an ambitious young man or woman, as it very often leads to management. But it is not, and is never likely to be, a stepping-stone to criticism. Press agents are paid

servants of the theatre, which puts them outside the critical
pale for ever. Happily—in this country, at any rate—criticism
is astonishingly honest. Managers may give lunches and cock-
tail-parties; but the only way to "buy" a critic is to buy the
paper—and even that does not always succeed. One effect
of the coming of the Press agent has been to make the collection
of any other theatrical news than that officially given out a
still more undesirable side-line for a critic.

Film Criticism

In the same way, the criticism of films does not fit in well
with that of plays. I did both for twelve years and am astonished
at having survived. It is not only that the combination means
working treble times—a film in the morning, a film in the
afternoon, a play in the evening, with writing and fussing in
between, and, if one is lucky, six hours' sleep. Alike the
technique and the standards of taste are so different that one
tends to become cynical and disinterested. It is idle, too, to
pretend that there are not, and will not always be, points of
antagonism between the two as business-interests. This makes
it inevitable that a critic who is human should be prejudiced,
consciously or not, according to the policy of the paper he
represents. If he is not so, or prejudiced in a contrary direction,
his position is even more uncomfortable.

Novel-writing, as I have already noted, is favoured in some
quarters. But the writer of a best-seller, like the winner of a
Derby sweep, must be treated as an exception. The writing of
unsuccessful or moderately successful hack-novels—or, indeed,
novels of any sort—seems generally to be much better done
where there is freedom to move about the world and get local
colour. A perpetual danger arrives with the need for returning
every night in thought and fact to the footlights and Fleet
Street. Indeed, it is almost bound to mean a novel about
the theatre after a year or two, and the consequent end either
of good novel-writing or of good daily criticism.

From a journalistic point of view, I have found book-
reviewing a better side-line than most; but even there I should
avoid the reviewing of novels—and they represent the staple of
so-called "literary" criticism. If they are conscientiously read

in any number—I have found a weekly half-dozen more than enough—they tend to stale dramatic perception. One gets weary of plots and of fiction in any form, which is unfair to the play one is going to see in the evening.

The Shared Critic

As for the writing of dramatic criticism for more than two or at most three newspapers, I have found this the worst form of critical drudgery. At one time I used to have to write five notices of every play. By the time it came to the last—especially as half a dozen or so other plays would have been produced in between—I usually wished the whole thing at kingdom-come. This is, I fear, a state of mind very prevalent in one form or another in present-day criticism. It is, perhaps, partly responsible for the habit of veering off the play under supposed consideration in aftermath notices. Certainly it is an attitude not likely to be helpful to dramatists, to actors, to managers, or to the public.

I have set these points down here because they are important to the young man or woman who is seriously bent upon becoming a regular, daily dramatic critic. The reason is that, although it can easily be made a whole-time job, dramatic criticism is not—and probably never will be—a whole-pay job for anyone who has not made a big name elsewhere. The number of staff-critics in London who are making more than £800 a year out of dramatic criticism alone for a single daily or evening paper could be tapped out with one's fingers. On weeklies I have known clever, highly-cultured men who had forfeited fine opportunities in other fields and had struggled to keep up a dress-suit existence, in the days when that was necessary, on £3 a week or less. Some have ended their lives in dire poverty—in harness to the finish. A very large number of periodicals have given up looking upon dramatic criticism as a professional affair at all—always, it may be said, with disastrous results to the product. A famous London weekly review was recently offering 10s. a page!

Education

In these circumstances I would suggest to the potential dramatic critic that he should arrange his other work from the

first and regard the representing of a national paper at anything like an adequate professional salary as, at best, an off-
chance. In my own case the temptation happened, as I have
described, very early and very easily. When I was appointed
dramatic critic of *The Morning Leader* on the strength of my
gallery-impression of Forbes-Robertson's Hamlet, the salary
was £3 a week. It remained so for seven years. I looked upon
the experience as an education, and cheerfully saw my young
colleagues going up to far more lucrative positions and distinguishing themselves both in Fleet Street and by transfer to
other professions.

An education it certainly was. It gave me the personal
friendship of Shaw, Archer, Walkley, Grein, and others of the
men who were making the dramatic criticism of the day
memorable and inspiring. It gave me the chance of seeing all
the plays of the later 'nineties—of seeing the rise of Shaw as a
dramatist, and of Barrie, and all the best work of Pinero,
Jones, Carton, Esmond, Marshall, and St. John Hankin, and
of Maugham from his first play onwards. It gave a whole
decade of Irving, with Hare, Wyndham, Hawtrey, the Kendals,
Forbes-Robertson, Tree, Alexander, and other now departed
actor-managers, all in their glory. It gave me the annual
seasons of Coquelin, Bernhardt, Réjane, Duse, and Ada
Rehan—not forgetting occasional visits of the *Comédie Française*
company, with Silvain and Féraudy, and a host of other
enlightenments. Admirable education as all this could not
help being, I soon found what all critics must find—that
without further purpose the end is just continued education.
The time comes when a new generation of young men are glad
to be educated at a small salary—I have seen several such waves
—and no editor pays more than he has got to. So there is
always a tendency for dramatic criticism as a profession to be
standardized in general at the lowest figure a young man
will take to be educated.

For Young Critics

In a way there is little to regret in this. So long as their
elders find an adequate market for their experience, no better
training could be imagined for young critics than daily work

with the responsibility of a large circulation to keep them from
going off into wild fallacies. Still, some little hints, born of
long service, may be useful. There are certain twists of mind
incident to youth—I myself was terribly guilty—which need
to be constantly kept in check.

One of the chief of these is the temptation to sneer, and to
court cheap notoriety by those spiteful epigrams which are so
easily concocted. They help nobody. They do not instruct
old playgoers or make new ones. In the end they are certain
to bring their revenges upon the critic himself. At the same
time, absolute candour, sincerity, and independence are
essential. I have always remembered the dictum of one of
my earliest and most respected editors. "Say just what you
like, my boy," he used to tell me, "so long as you sincerely
think it and have reason for the faith that is in you. I don't
mind who it is you go for. All I ask is that you should be glad
if the play is a good one and sorry if it is not." How natural
and reasonable a point of view it seems! Yet I have again
and again known young critics—and not only young ones—
hailing some ghastly failure delightedly, as giving them scope
for throwing paper-pellets with impunity. This sort of thing
only gets dramatic criticism into disrepute, without betraying
an attractive personality in the critic.

Let satire say what it will, dramatic criticism more than
any other—on account of its intensely practical effect—should
be constructive rather than destructive. If destruction is deserved, criticism can be convincing only when it is known that
the critic is a true lover of the theatre and not given to unneces-
sary attack. By constructive criticism I mean that which
encourages good and struggling work, builds up reputations
by persistent interest, interprets ideas that might be misunder-
stood, creates in the reader a wish for what is best in the
theatre, and offers, without impertinent intrusion, an occasional
suggestion of new possibilities.

Young critics may, none the less, be warned against a kind
of "constructive" criticism which is boring to everybody and
of no use to the theatre. This is the harping upon niggling and
purely technical matters—little points of setting, construction,
or stage-management—which would often be far better dealt

with in a letter to, or talk with, the producer, playwright, or actor. It is the besetting sin of many young academic critics, desirous of revealing a nascent understanding of play-craft. I myself have found it well to keep always in mind that in a national newspaper one is writing not for the theatrical manager but for a public spread over the entire kingdom, most of whom will not even see the play and are only confused by contentions over trifles.

Amateur Movement

At this point it may be well to turn to some phases of present-day criticism in different circumstances. Whatever happens in the columns of modern national newspapers, congested with a thousand more clamant interests, dramatic criticism is growing more active than ever in other quarters. The provincial papers still offer a ready field for the competent journalist who is not dependent upon the theatre alone for his livelihood. Manchester, Liverpool, and Birmingham have each a great critical tradition and sustain it. Most of the larger provincial papers give longer notices to visiting productions than that with which the London original was—or will be—favoured. Even the paragraph in a provincial "London Letter" often affords a better idea of a West-End play than is to be found from what should be more authoritative sources. The writers of these are no less dramatic critics because they have other affairs to concern them. In all sorts of out-of-the-way places I have found criticism fostering revival of the living drama, where until recently every vestige of it had been swept away.

The amateur movement is offering a new and almost unlimited task to dramatic critics. The work of competition-judges and lecturers frequently reveals a breadth of view, an eagerness, and a sense of delight in pioneer creation which puts to shame those half-hearted professional references to trashy farce or doubtful comedy that one knows so well. The word "amateur" must connote nowadays all that is done for joy in the work itself and not for exploitation. I should include many enterprises that do not come strictly under the amateur label. I should include, for instance, part-time repertory companies, like that of the Maddermarket at Norwich. These semi-amateur repertory companies have been, and still are, immensely important seeding-grounds for the new professional theatre now springing to life again after the temporary deluge of cinema-and-radio competition.

Creation

In days gone by the amateur stage was, as many of us remember only too well, almost wholly imitative and therefore seldom worth critical notice. We had a galaxy of accepted dramatists on the professional stage—very occasionally added to by some managerial "discovery." Their plays were regularly presented at appropriate West-End theatres, then went on tour, were finally released for amateur performance, and were duly repeated by a cluster of well-known amateur clubs. This routine-phase of amateur production is by no means dead. Many of the old clubs, such as the Old Stagers and the Windsor Strollers, still honourably survive. The ever-growing number of amateur dramatic and operatic societies belonging to banks and business-houses still rush for every successful musical play and popular comedy as it becomes available. They still keep up the vogue of Gilbert and Sullivan, and they afford a stable income to the author of any moderately bright play which has a long cast of fairly equal and easy character-parts.

The outlook is altogether different in regard to the creative amateur. He has been responsible, one way and another, for nearly everything that is worth while on our present stage. From Stanislavski and the Moscow Art Theatre, Antoine's *Théâtre Libre*, the New York Theatre Guild, and our own Independent Theatre and Stage Society—amateur in spirit for all their professional casts—to the host of organizations now gathered under the British Drama League's banner, what our stage and the stage of the world owe to work that has been done without thought of profit has been incalculable.

William Poel

It is in the encouragement of amateur production of this order that criticism has had—and still has—a great duty to perform. The late William Poel, for instance, and the productions of his Elizabethan Stage Society happened to coincide with my early days as a dramatic critic. From the standpoint of popular interest—a standpoint which some modern newspapers regard with a kind of statistical reverence, apportioning their attention in exact ratio to the numbers present—they were of no value whatever. Here were a few hundred rather crankish people gathered in a city-hall, seeing something utterly at variance with every canon of current attractiveness. The performances were given in a dim light and to the accompaniment of obsolete musical instruments. If there had been no critic impelled to let the world know that at the back of it all was something which was right where everything else was wrong, nothing more would have happened. Fortunately a few critics—I can proudly confess to having been one of them— were so impressed that they defied their own professional interests by writing quite a deal about Poel. The result was that though he himself benefited not at all—not being of an exploitatory turn of mind—his ideas gradually spread. He proved, in a phrase actually used by Granville Barker, "good to steal from."

So also with Gordon Craig—whom I would include in my encomiums were it not that a long friendship convinces me he would resent furiously being referred to as having anything to do with "amateurs." Among others, Reinhardt was inspired by both Craig and Poel to make profitable havoc of accepted conventions in theatres little and big. Thus it came about that although only a comparative handful of enthusiasts saw those early productions of Poel and Craig—Poel's were presented at an average cost of £150 each, much of which came out of his own pocket—no Shakespearian or classic production of any kind would be tolerated nowadays which did not owe some quality to them. The Poel production of *Everyman*, to which I have already referred, established a modern miracle-play tradition, which made Cochran's great show at Olympia possible. It has had comparatively recent fruit in such exquisite things as Charles Claye's *A Joyous Pageant of the Holy Nativity*—another wholly amateur production— played to crowded audiences in every kind of building, from cathedral to music-hall.

Apostolate of Critics

I need not go through the long list of all the amateur enter-prises which have owed their wider influence upon the theatre in general to intelligent and sympathetic criticism. Practically every new vista that has opened, and is opening, has been due to this *entente* between the creative amateur and such critics as are not content with the mere recording of self-evident success. It was so from the early days of the Independent Theatre to the arrival of Shaw as a "commercial dramatist." It was so from the starting of the little amateur group which preceded the Abbey Theatre in Dublin to the presenting of Synge's *The Playboy of the Western World* and O'Casey's *Juno and the Paycock*. It was so from the founding of the Mermaid Society by a critic, Philip Carr, to its direct outcome in Sir Nigel Playfair's management of the Lyric, Hammersmith, and from the Pilgrim Players to Sir Barry Jackson's estab-lishment of the Birmingham Repertory Theatre. In all of these and countless other enterprises, which began with faith and led—some of them—to fortune, the apostolate of critics has been undeniable.

It is happening still all over England and America, wherever there is an amateur or semi-amateur theatre doing the kind of work those pioneers of other days set before them. But it is not happening to the extent one would wish. This is partly because dramatic endeavour—above all, amateur endeavour —is getting more and more localized, while newspaper-interest is being more and more centralized. Though some provincial papers do, as I have said, pay considerable attention to visiting London stars, they tend to be briefer and less impassioned over the achievements of their neighbours. Perhaps this is inevitable —"a prophet is not without honour, save in his own country"— but the more adventurous kind of amateur theatre in a provin-cial town has thereby a harder struggle than it need have.

Again and again on journeying to a provincial town to see a performance of genuine importance from an artistic point of view I have opened the local paper to find very little about the event. But there will be columns of palpable "blurb," sent round from the London publicity office, about stale American films which have been done to death elsewhere and have no local bearing whatsoever. Sometimes I feel that it is not always the newspaper's fault. I have known young theatre-managers settle in a town and imagine that the local journalists are going to form a worshipping choir immediately of their own accord. This is, it must be emphasized, not the habit of local or any other journalists. Before these "chartered libertines" show respect they very naturally demand respect.

Reporter

If the editors themselves can be wooed and won to forget the inevitable commercial preponderance of other attractions, well and good. It has been done miraculously in some instances. But the local critic has to be recognized as such. Though he is called a reporter and may not always be in evening-dress, to express open disappointment to his face because he does not happen to be a big man with a big name from London is always unwise. Even if he is a young fellow whose knowledge is assumed rather than acquired, it is for the manager to go down on his knees, and thank Heaven fasting for a good journalist's love. The junior reporter is never to be despised. He may be a proprietor in a year or two. At the worst he also can learn—and like it.

When all else fails, there is no questioning the value of the critical programme or theatre-magazine—though this is apt to dwindle into a "who's who" of the cast. The precedent of Lessing is rarely followed except in some university-magazines, where we do get a certain amount of candid analysis of the play and its treatment. I myself am a great believer in amateur critics for amateur actors. But the theatre-magazine cannot, and never will, replace the unhampered criticism of an independent newspaper. This is preferable not only because the critic is then in a position to administer reproof, but because he can dare to be far more outspoken in his praise.

The best arrangement is when a little body of theatre-folk and local critics are all working and hoping and dreaming together, moved by a common bond of love of the theatre and of their native or adopted home. It leads to that pride in common achievement which is one of the chief delights in theatre-work of all kinds. This was one of the happy characteristics of the old

Horniman days in Manchester. Beneath all the grime of the black-faced old city one felt that it was good "in that dawn to be alive." In the circumstances, how easy to forgive an apparent forgetfulness sometimes that what Manchester thought to-day England had thought some three-hundred-odd years before!

Within recent years the extension of film criticism and radio criticism and ballet criticism into specialized departments has undoubtedly had a narrowing effect upon the outlook of the "old-fashioned" dramatic critic. The music critic, too, is more ready than he used to be to enlarge the salient of grand opera, and to claim all kinds of drama with music as within his province. These are, of course, comparatively trivial details. If they relieve the dramatic critic of work for which he has not time, and do not interfere too much with the space accorded him for productions where there is no doubt about the predominant element—and there are more than enough of these in London alone to keep one man busy every day of his life—no harm is done. In so far as specialized experts in music, films, and broadcasting deal with drama they are dramatic critics. Any questions between accepted colleagues hardly enter into our present considerations. It is enough that everybody who calls himself a dramatic critic should use his best endeavours to know and understand all forms of dramatic appeal.

A Larger Life

In any case it is clear that if the responsibility of dramatic criticism is being contended for it is something of power and importance—probably of growing power and importance. Whoever the critic is, and in whatever direction his specialized knowledge may be, he is still a "guardian of the aesthetic fact." Nor is he only the guardian. He is also at once the herald and the questioner of that whole mystery of make-believe, in the inner meaning of which forty centuries have made hardly more difference than forty years. It is possible that social changes may have a certain effect upon the theatre itself—in the exclusive significance of the word. The cinema drove drama out of the theatre for a time in many quarters; but it had curiously little power to change it, and broadcasting none whatever. Television is not likely to do much more than both together, either as an influence or as a rival. These are not human expressions in the same sense as a stage-play. They do not need the human response which true criticism conveys and inspires. At the same time I do foresee a partial emergence from what is still to so great an extent the eighteenth-century tradition in the theatre itself. I fancy we may find not so many drawing-room comedies for drawing-room theatres, and more broad treatments of a larger life, with studies of racial character and the world-scene, better informed than those provided by present-day revue and so-called romance.

What effect the National Theatre, of which the Queen Mother has so graciously laid the foundation-stone, will have on this remains to be seen. I have already dealt with its practical side. As one of the few remaining original promoters of the scheme, and a member of the committee for more than a quarter of a century, I need hardly reassert my already expressed belief that it will be of great benefit not only to the theatre at large but to criticism. As yet—even after the royally honoured building is completed—I do not think it would be wise to expect too much pioneering adventure from the National Theatre. There must still be real life and movement in the theatres elsewhere to make it even possible. The principal value of the National Theatre will be in co-ordinating and extending the splendid work already accomplished and still in progress toward setting a standard in the presentation of Shakespeare and of the ever-growing body of British drama which should not be allowed to die.

Dignity

A National Theatre will also give dignity to the drama as an art, as something of abiding value to the character of the nation. It has been said that all this could be done without setting up a new theatre, and that an organization without a playhouse of its own would be just as useful. In this may be detected at once the old, familiar accent of hostility to the theatre and to any effort of any kind on its behalf. Why not set up a new theatre? As it happens, Great Britain is small enough—as Stratford on Avon has shown us—for an actual theatre to be visitable at pretty frequent intervals from all parts of the kingdom. In America the distances are so much greater that one building could hardly bear the same relation to the whole. The record of the Federal Theatre told us, during its now-abandoned adventure, what can be managed under government auspices by people who have faith in their purpose and its future. Starting as it did by way of an industrial experiment for the employment of out-of-work actors, it might have discovered all over the United States a fresh market for new and old material at popular prices. This would have been all to the good; but a very different thing is the establishing of a standard of achievement in one central theatre. Despite all difficulties, many enterprises on the idealistic, uncommercial plane prove clearly enough that the flesh-and-blood theatre is very far from being a dead or even dying interest. The enormous popularity of ballet has not, perhaps, done much as yet to help the spoken drama, but it may do so in the end. After all, it was out of ballet that drama grew ages ago—and human nature has altered astonishingly little in the meantime.

Somerset Maugham's jeremiad over the prospects of so-called "realistic" drama in his book, *The Summing Up*, seems to me to mistake the foreground for the horizon. He writes—

> I cannot but state my belief that the prose-drama to which I have given so much of my life will soon be dead. . . . Perhaps the best chance the realistic dramatist has to-day is to occupy himself with what, till now, at all events, the screen has not succeeded very well in presenting—the drama in which the action is inner rather than outer, and the comedy of wit. . . . To my mind, the drama took a wrong turning when the demand for realism led it to abandon the ornament of verse. Verse has a specific dramatic value, as anyone can see by observing in himself the thrilling effect of a tirade in one of Racine's plays or of any of Shakespeare's great set pieces; and this is independent of the sense. It is due to the emotional power of rhythmical speech. But more than that . . . verse delivers a play from sober reality. It puts it on a higher level, at one remove from life, and so makes it easier for the audience to attune themselves to that state of feeling in which they are most susceptible to the drama's specific appeal.

Tradition

All this is, of course, as any reader of Somerset Maugham's book will remember, largely due to the fact that its author was

at that time confessedly tired of the frictional and often dis-
heartening work which even the most successful dramatist has
to face in order to get his ideas presented on the stage. He was,
he tells us, tired even of the public whom he saw queueing
to see his own plays. His right and wise suggestion as regards a
return to verse has already been partly fulfilled in the success
of *Murder in the Cathedral* and other verse-dramas. I doubt very
much the need for announcing final obsequies even of the
realistic prose-play. Just at the moment the English-speaking
public may not be in a mood for the particular type of closely
psychological and rather cynical comedy which Somerset
Maugham supplied in his mature years. But this need not
prevent or discount the arrival of new dramatists of genius in
that kind, full of energy and of apparently fresh ideas. The
true history of the drama goes forward in cycles represented
not by decades but by aeons. It took, as we have seen, two
thousand years to prepare for the Elizabethan outburst. The
Greek dramatists were the fruit of a period longer still. On
the surface is perpetual change in accordance with the externals of civilization. The essentials alter almost imperceptibly
with centuries. In modern-dress performances of Shakespeare,
on both sides of the Atlantic, we find that the only consequent
troubles which really count are a few archaic words, the
absence of telephones and cars—easily brought in—and the
carrying of swords. Otherwise how little three hundred years
matter!

Nearly all supposed new movements are just the picking
up of temporarily forgotten traditions—never exactly as they
were, but with that slight difference which marks humanity's
general struggle to larger knowledge and more widespread
comfort. Living drama is particularly liable to seem reaction-
ary, bound as it is by the physical presence of actor and audience. The "expressionistic" stage, for instance, has been much
in vogue lately, with its neglect of detailed imitation and
imposed moral purpose. It goes back, through Nietzsche, to
the old Dionysian rites and revels. Yet it affords what appears
to be a new freedom. It gives a means by which "news" and
discussion can be brought—as they were in the age of Aeschylus
and Euripides—within the domain of dramatic art. How

much of Shaw's time would have been saved if he had not had, in his early days, to box up his ideas within the four walls of realistic comedy! So long as we live and move physically and meet one another's real-life selves, I believe flesh-and-blood drama will survive. It and the criticism that goes with it will at their best be a perpetual reminder of ideal beauty on the one hand and of how far—but never entirely—humanity falls short of that ideal. It will help us to explore the unknown world of fancy and the known world of all times and places. It will give us tears for the sorrows of others and, in them, forgetfulness of our own. It will bring to us the divine gift of laughter without malice and without abasement. It will blend all these together in a simulacrum—whether "realistic" or not—of the eternal movement and contrast which make so large a part of life's magic.

Seven Lamps

One might summarize these elements of what is good in the theatre as seven lamps, the tending of which is part of the task of dramatic criticism. They would be faith, truth, imagination, knowledge, sympathy, humour, variety. The greatest of these is faith. We have always to remember that the theatre, whether grave or gay, is still in many respects—as it was once entirely—a place of worship. What is called "illusion" is an act of prayer. We seek out what we really want—be it coarse fun or tragic pathos or moral challenge—and we ask to be helped to imagine it true for us. This is at the heart of all the living drama's problems and strange responses. It is this that distinguishes the active playgoer, with his turbulent expressions of judgment or enthusiasm, from the devotee of other arts. He or she goes to the theatre, not for passive entertainment, but for personal and communal expression of passionate belief in some view of life. It may be light-hearted or fiercely emotional. It may be cynical or even grossly materialistic. The critic who records, and to the best of his ability guides, these waves of public sentiment or mirth or intellectual approval in what he honestly believes to be a right direction can hardly have laboured in vain.

BIBLIOGRAPHY

ADAMS, W. DAVENPORT: *A Book of Burlesque* (1891).

ADDISON, JOSEPH: *The Spectator, No.* 419 (1712); *Remarks Upon Italy* (1705).

AESCHYLUS: *Agamemnon*, trans. by Louis MacNeice (1936); *The Suppliant Woman*, trans. by Gilbert Murray (1930); *Prometheus Bound*, trans. by Gilbert Murray (1931); *Prometheus Bound*, trans. by T. G. Tucker (1935).

AGATE, JAMES: *The English Dramatic Critics*, ed. (1932).

ALBRIGHT, EVELYN MAY: *Dramatic Publication in England, 1580–1640* (1927).

AMERICAN ANTIQUITIES IN THE BRITISH MUSEUM (Short Guide) (1912).

ARCHER, WILLIAM: *The Theatrical World* (1896); *William Charles Macready* (1890); *Playmaking* (1913).

ARISTOPHANES: *Comedies*, trans. by W. J. Hickie (1853); *The Frogs*, trans. by Gilbert Murray (1908).

ARISTOTLE: *Poetic*, trans. by Theodore Buckley (1872).

ARMSTRONG, C. F.: *A Century of Great Actors* (1912).

ARNOLD, MATTHEW: *Essays in Criticism* (First and Second Series) (1865 and 1888).

ASTON, W. G.: *A History of Japanese Literature* (1898).

AUBREY, JOHN: *Miscellanies* (1696).

AUGUSTINE, ST.: *The City of God*, trans. by John Healey (1931).

BACON, DELIA: *The Philosophy of the Plays of Shakespeare Unfolded* (1857).

BAKSHY, ALEXANDER: *The Path of the Modern Russian Stage* (1916).

BANCROFT, SIR S. AND LADY: *Mr. and Mrs. Bancroft* (1889).

BARKER, HARLEY GRANVILLE: *A National Theatre* (1930).

BERTRAND, LOUIS: *St. Augustine* (1914).

BETTERTON, THOMAS: *The History of the English Stage from the Restoration* (1741).

BOAS, F. S.: *Tudor Drama* (1933); *Shakespeare and His Predecessors* (1896); *Medwall's "Fulgens and Lucres"* (1926); *Marlowe and His Circle* (1929).

BRADLEY, A. C.: *Shakespearean Tragedy* (1909).

BRERETON, AUSTIN: *The Life of Henry Irving* (1908).

BROADBENT, R. J.: *A History of Pantomime* (1901).

BROOKE, C. F. TUCKER: *The Tudor Drama* (1912).

BROWN, IVOR: *Shakespeare* (1949).

BROWNING, ELIZABETH BARRETT: *Poems* (1844).

BUDGE, SIR ERNEST WALLIS: *Osiris and the Egyptian Resurrection* (1891); *The Literature of the Ancient Egyptians* (1914).

BYRON, LORD: *English Bards and Scotch Reviewers* (1809).

CAMPBELL, LEWIS: *A Guide to Greek Tragedy* (1891).

CANNON, W. W.: *The Song of Songs* (1913).

CARTER, HUNTLY: *The Theatre of Max Reinhardt* (1914); *The New Spirit in the Russian Theatre*, 1917–28 (1929).

CELLIER, FRANÇOIS, AND BRIDGEMAN, CUNNINGHAM: *Gilbert, Sullivan, and D'Oyly Carte* (1927).

CERVANTES, MIGUEL DE: *Don Quixote,* trans. by J. Ormsby (1885).

CHAMBERS, SIR EDMUND: *The Medieval Stage* (1903); *The Elizabethan Stage* (1923); *William Shakespeare* (1930); *English Pastorals*, ed. (1895).

CHANDLER, FRANK W.: *Modern Continental Playwrights* (1931).

CHISHOLM, CECIL: *Repertory* (1934).

CHURCHILL, CHARLES: *The Rosciad* (1781).

CIBBER, COLLEY: *An Apology for the Life of Mr. Colley Cibber*, ed. by Robert W. Lowe (1889).

COHEN, GUSTAVE: *Le Miracle de Théophile; Le Jeu de Robin et Marion;* and *Le Jeu d'Adam et Eve* (1934–6).

COLERIDGE, S. T.: *Lectures and Notes on Shakespeare*, ed. by T. Ashe (1883); "Principle of Method" in *The Friend* (1818).

COLLINS, CLIFTON W.: *Sophocles* (1886).

COLLINS, W. LUCAS: *Plautus and Terence* (1873).

COOK, DUTTON: *A Book of the Play* (1876).

COPERNICUS, NICOLAS: *De Revolutionibus Orbium Coelestium* (1543).

CORNEILLE, PIERRE: *Œuvres* (Vol. 12) (1862).

CORNFORD, FRANCIS M.: *The Origin of Attic Comedy* (1914).

CORVAT, THOMAS: *Crudities* (1611).

COURTHOPE, W. J.: *History of English Poetry* (1910).

CRAIG, EDWARD GORDON: *On the Art of the Theatre* (1911).

CREIZENACH, WILLIAM: *The English Drama in the Age of Shakespeare*, trans. (1916).

CROCE, BENEDETTO: *Ariosto, Shakespeare and Corneille*, trans. by Douglas Ainslie (1921).

DAVIES, ROBERT: *Extracts from the Municipal Records of York* (1843).

DEANE, CECIL V.: *Dramatic Theory and the Rhymed Heroic Play* (1931).

DEBURAU, GASPARD AND CHARLES: *Pantomimes* (1889).

DEMBLON, C.: *Lord Rutland est Shakespeare* (1913).

DENT, EDWARD J.: *Foundations of English Opera* (1928).

DE QUINCEY, T.: *Collected Writings*, ed. by D. Masson (1889–90).

DIBDIN, T. J.: *Reminiscences* (1827).

DICKENS, CHARLES: *The Life of Charles James Mathews* (1879); *Memoirs of Joseph Grimaldi*, ed. by "Boz" (1838).

DICKINSON, THOMAS H.: *Playwrights of the New American Theatre* (1925).

DIDEROT, DENIS: *Paradoxe sur le Comédien* (1784).

DISHER, M. WILLSON: *Clowns and Pantomimes* (1925).

D'ISRAELI, ISAAC: *Curiosities of Literature* (1834).

DOBRÉE, BONAMY: *Restoration Tragedy* (1929).
DONALDSON, JOHN WILLIAM: *The Theatre of the Greeks* (1836).
DONNELLY, IGNATIUS: *The Great Cryptogram* (1888).
DORAN, JOHN: *Annals of the English Stage*, ed. by Robert W. Lowe (1888).
DOWDEN, EDWARD: *Shakespeare: His Mind and Art*. (1875).
DOWNS, HAROLD: *Theatre and Stage*, ed. (1934).
DRYDEN, JOHN: *Essays*, ed. by W. P. Ker (1900); *Essay on Dramatick Poesy* (1668).
DUKES, ASHLEY: "The English Scene" in *Theatre Arts Monthly* (1934); *Modern Dramatists* (1911).

ELWIN, MALCOLM: *The Playgoer's Handbook to Restoration Drama* (1928).
ETHNOGRAPHICAL COLLECTIONS IN THE BRITISH MUSEUM (Handbook) (1910).
EURIPIDES: *The Cyclops*, trans. by Percy Bysshe Shelley (1824).

FARRELL, LEWIS R.: *The Cults of the Greek States* (1909).
FENELLOSA, ERNEST, AND POUND, EZRA: *Noh, or Accomplishment* (1916).
FRENCH, MRS. YVONNE: *Mrs. Siddons: Tragic Actress* (1937).
FIELDING, HENRY: *Works*, ed. by George Saintsbury (1893).
FILON, AUGUSTIN: *The English Stage*, trans. by Frederick Whyte (1897).
FITZGERALD, EDWARD: *Six Dramas of Calderon* (1853).
FLANAGAN, HALLIE: *Shifting Scenes of the Modern European Theatre* (1929).
FORBES-ROBERTSON, SIR JOHNSON: *An Actor Under Three Reigns* (1925).
FRANCE, ANATOLE: *La Vie Littéraire* (Preface) (1888).
FRAZER, SIR JAMES: *The Golden Bough* (1900); *Adonis, Attis, Osiris* (1907).
FRIEDLANDER, LUDWIG: *Roman Life and Manners Under the Early Empire*, trans. (1908).
FURNIVALL, F. J.: *The Royal Shakespeare* (1894).
FYFE, W. H.: *The Poetics of Aristotle*, with trans. (1927).

GALILEI, GALILEO: *Siderius Nuncius* (1610).
GALLUP, MRS.: *The Bi-Lateral Cipher of Francis Bacon* (1900).
GAYLEY, CHARLES MILLS: *Representative English Comedies* (1903).
GENEST, JOHN: *Some Account of the English Stage* (1832).
GIBBON, EDWARD: *The Decline and Fall of the Roman Empire* (1776-88).
GILES, HERBERT A.: *History of Chinese Literature* (1901).
GOETHE: *Conversations with Eckermann*, trans. by John Oxenford (1850).
GOSSE, SIR EDMUND: *Seventeenth Century Studies* (1897).
GOSSON, STEPHEN: *Schoole of Abuse* (1579).
GRAY, THOMAS: *Pindaric Odes* (1758).

GREEK AND ROMAN LIFE AT THE BRITISH MUSEUM (Guide) (1920).
GREENE, ROBERT: *Works*, ed. by Alexander Grosart (1881–6).
GREG, W. W.: *Pastoral Poetry and Pastoral Drama* (1906).
GREIN, J. T.: *Dramatic Criticism* (1902).
GROTE, GEORGE,: *A History of Greece* (1846–56).

HAIGH, A. E.: *The Attic Theatre* (1889).
HALL, DR. H. R.: *The Civilization of the Philistines* (Cambridge Universal History).
HARRISON, JANE ELLEN: *Themis* (1912).
HAUPTMANN, GERHART: *Dramatic Works*, ed. by Ludwig Lewisohn (1913).
HAVENEYER, DR. L.: *The Drama of Savage Peoples* (1916).
HAWKINS, F. W.: *Life of Edmund Kean* (1869).
HAZLITT, WILLIAM: *Characters of Shakespeare's Plays* (1817); *Criticisms and Dramatic Essays* (1851).
HERFORD, C. H., AND SIMPSON, PERCY: *Ben Jonson : The Man and His Work* (1925).
HERODOTUS: *History*, trans. by George Rawlinson (1880).
HEYWOOD, JOHN: *Works*, ed. by J. S. Farmer (1905–6).
HEYWOOD, THOMAS: *Hierarchie of the Blessed Angels* (1635); *Apology for Actors* (1612).
HOLCROFT, THOMAS: "Mrs. Siddons" in *The English Review* (1783).
HOLLINGSHEAD, JOHN: *My Lifetime* (1895); *Gaiety Chronicles* (1898).
HONE, WILLIAM: *Ancient Mysteries Described* (1823).
HORACE: *Epistles and Art of Poetry*, trans. by James Lonsdale and Samuel Lee (1881).
HORRWITZ, R. P.: *The Indian Theatre* (1912).
HOWE, PERCIVAL P.: *The Repertory Theatre* (1910).
HSIUNG, S. J.: *Lady Precious Stream* (1934).

IBSEN, HENRIK: *Collected works*, ed. with introduction by William Archer (1907); *Theatrical World* for 1893–7.
INCHBALD, MRS.: *Memoirs*, ed. by John Boaden (1833).

JACKSON, SIR BARRY V.: *The Marvellous History of St. Bernard*, adapted by Henri Ghéon, trans. (1925).
JANIN, JULES: *Deburau: L'Histoire du Théâtre à Quatre Sous* (1832).
JASTROW, MORRIS: *The Book of Job; Its Origin, Growth and Interpretation* (1920).
JEBB, SIR RICHARD: *Essays and Addresses* (1907).
JERROLD, WALTER: *Douglas Jerrold* (1918).
JEVONS, F. B.: *A History of Greek Literature* (1886).
JOHNSON, SAMUEL: *The Dramatic Writings of William Shakespeare* (Preface) (1765).
JONES, HENRY ARTHUR: *The Foundations of National Drama* (1913).
JONSON, BEN: *Discoveries*, ed. by Henry Morley (1889).

JUSSERAND, J.: *Le Théâtre en Angleterre* (1881).
JUVENAL: *Satires*, trans. by G. G. Ramsay (1918).

KALIDASA: *Sakuntala, or The Fatal Ring*, trans. by Sir William Jones (1789); *Sakuntala*, trans. by T. Holme (1902); *The Little Clay Cart*, trans. by A. W. Ryder (1905).
KEITH, A. BERRIEDALE: *The Sanskrit Drama* (1924).
KELLY, J. F.: *Lope de Vega and the Spanish Drama* (1902).
KEPLER, JOHANN: *Astronomia Nova* (1609).
KNIGHT, JOSEPH: *David Garrick* (1894).
KNOX, A. D.: *Mimes and Fragments*, trans. and ed. (1929).
KOMISARJEVSKY, THEODORE: *Myself and the Theatre* (1929).

LAMB, CHARLES: *Essays of Elia* (1823); *Dramatic Essays*, ed. by Brander Matthews (1891).
LAWRENCE, ARTHUR: *Journalism as a Profession* (1903).
LEE, SIR SIDNEY: *The Life of Shakespeare* (rev. ed. 1915).
LEE, VERNON: *Eighteenth Century Studies* (1907).
LEFRANC, A.: *Sous le Masque de "W. S."* (1919).
LEIGH HUNT, JAMES HENRY: Essays from *The Indicator* (1879); *Dramatic Essays*, ed. by William Archer and Robert W. Lowe (1895).
LESSING, GOTTHOLD EPHRAIM: *Selected Prose Works*, trans. by G. Edward Bell (1890); *Dramatic Notes*, trans. and ed. by G. Edward Bell (1900).
LEVI, SYLVAIN: *Le Théâtre Indien* (1890).
LEWES, GEORGE HENRY: *The Spanish Drama* (1846); *On Actors and the Art of Acting* (1875).
LICHTENBERG, G. C.: *Auserlesene Schriften*, trans. (1770).
LITTLEWOOD, S. R.: *Elizabeth Inchbald and Her Circle* (1921); *The Story of Pierrot* (1911); *An Anthology of Modern Drama*, ed. (1936).
LOMBARD, FRANK A.: *The Japanese Drama* (1928).
LONGINUS: *On the Sublime*, trans. and ed. by W. Rhys Roberts (1899).
LOONEY, T.: *Shakespeare Identified* (1920).
LUCIAN: *De Saltatione*, trans. by H. W. and F. G. Fowler (1905).
LYLY, JOHN: *Complete Works*, ed. by R. W. Bond (1902).
LYTTON, THE EARL OF: *Life of the First Lord Lytton* (1913).

MACAULAY, LORD: *Essays: Historical and Literary* (1843).
MACCARTHY, DESMOND: *The Court Theatre, 1904–7* (1907).
MACDONELL, ARTHUR A.: *A History of Sanskrit Literature* (1900).
MACKAIL, J. W.: *The Approach to Shakespeare* (1930).
MACKENZIE, AGNES MURE: *The Playgoer's Handbook to the English Renaissance Drama* (1927).

MACREADY, WILLIAM CHARLES: *Reminiscences, Diaries and Letters*, ed. by Sir Frederick Pollock (1876).
MADDEN, D. H.: *The Diary of Master William Silence* (1907).
MAGNIN, CHARLES: *Les Origines du Théâtre Antique et du Théâtre Moderne* (1868).
MAINE, SIR HENRY SUMNER: *Ancient Law* (1887).
MALONE, ANDREW E.: *The Irish Drama* (1929).
MANTZIUS, KARL: *A History of Theatrical Art in Ancient and Modern Times*, trans. by Louise von Cossel (1903–9).
MARCELLINUS, AMMIANUS: *History of Rome*, trans. by C. U. Clark (1910).
MARTIN, SIR THEODORE: *Monographs: Garrick, Macready, Rachel* (1906).
MARTIN-HARVEY, SIR JOHN: *Autobiography* (1934).
MATTHEWS, BRANDER: *Shakespeare as a Playwright* (1913); *Playwrights on Playmaking* (1923).
MAUGHAM, W. SOMERSET: *Introduction to Plays* (1931–3); *The Summing Up* (1938).
MENANDER: *Principal Fragments*, trans. by Francis G. Allinson (1921).
MENCKEN, HENRY L.: *The Philosophy of Friedrich Nietzshe* (1908).
MEREDITH, GEORGE: *An Essay on Comedy* (1879).
MERES, FRANCIS: *Palladis Tamia: Wit's Treasury* (1598).
MILTON, JOHN: *Poetic Works*, ed. by David Masson (1890).
MOLIÈRE, JEAN BAPTISTE: *Plays*, ed. and trans. by A. R. Waller (1907).
MOULTON, RICHARD G.: *The Ancient Classical Drama* (1890).
MURRAY, GILBERT: *A History of Ancient Greek Literature* (1898); *Euripides and His Age* (1923); *Euripides: Verse Translations* (1902–14).

NASH, THOMAS: *Preface to Greene's "Menaphon"* (1589); *Works*, ed. by R. B. McKerrow (1904–10).
NATHAN, GEORGE JEAN: *The Critic and the Drama* (1922).
NICOLL, ALLARDYCE: *A History of Restoration Drama, 1660–1700* (1923); *A History of Early Eighteenth Century Drama, 1700–50* (1925); *A History of Early Eighteenth Century Drama 1750–1800* (1927); *A History of Early Nineteenth Century Drama, 1800–50* (1930); *The English Theatre* (1936).
NIETZSCHE, FRIEDRICH: *The Birth of Tragedy*, trans. by W. A. Haussmann (1909).
NOEL, HON. RODEN: *Otway's Plays* (Preface) (1888).
NORWOOD, GILBERT: *Greek Tragedy* (1920); *Greek Comedy* (1931).

OLIPHANT, MRS., AND TARVER, F.: *Molière* (1879).
ORME, MICHAEL (MRS. J. T. GREIN): *J. T. Grein: The Story of a Pioneer*, rev. by G. Bernard Shaw.

OTWAY, THOMAS: *Works*, ed. by Thomas Thornton (1813).
OVID: *Fasti and Tristia*, trans. by H. T. Riley (1851).

PALMER, JOHN: *Studies in the Contemporary Theatre* (1927).
PARRY, EDWARD ABBOTT: *Charles Macklin* (1891).
PATRIARCH OF ANTIOCH, THE: *Barlaam and Joséphat*, ed. by J. Jacobs (1896).
PEARCE, C. E.: *Madame Vestris and Her Times* (1923).
PEARSON, HESKETH: *The Life of Oscar Wilde* (1946).
PEELE, GEORGE: *The Arraignment of Paris*, ed. by O. Smeaton (1905); *The Old Wives' Tale*, ed. by A. H. Bullen (1888).
PEMBERTON, T. EDGAR: *The Life and Writings of T. W. Robertson* (1893).
PENDLEBURY, B. J.: *Dryden's Heroic Plays* (1923).
PEPYS, SAMUEL: *Diary* (1664–8).
PERRAULT, CHARLES: *Fairy Tales*, trans. and ed. by S. R. Littlewood (1912).
PETRONIUS: *Satyrion*, trans. by M. Heseltine (1913).
PICKARD-CAMBRIDGE, A. W.: *Dithyramb, Tragedy and Comedy* (1927).
PLANCHÉ, JAMES ROBINSON: *Recollections* (1872).
PLATO: *Symposium*, trans. by W. R. M. Lamb (1925).
PLAUTUS: *Comédies*, trans. by H. T. Riley (1880).
PLAYFAIR, SIR NIGEL: *The Story of the Lyric Theatre, Hammersmith* (1925).
PLUTARCH: *Lives*, trans. by B. Perrin (1914); *Moralia*, trans. by Harold North Fowler (1936).
POEL, WILLIAM: *Shakespeare in the Theatre* (1913).
POLLARD, A. W.: *English Miracle Plays* (1898).
POPE, ALEXANDER: *Preface to Shakespeare's Plays* (1725).
PRYNNE, WILLIAM: *Histrio-mastix* (1632).

QUINN, ARTHUR HOBSON: *A History of the American Drama* (1938).

RAWLINSON, GEORGE: *The Five Great Monarchies of the Ancient Eastern World* (1879).
RHYS, ERNEST: *"Everyman" and Other Interludes*, ed. (1909).
RIDGEWAY, SIR WILLIAM: *The Dramas and Dramatic Dances of Non-European Races* (1915); *The Origin of Tragedy* (1910).
ROBERTSON, J. G.: *Goethe* (1927).
ROBINSON, HENRY CRABB: *Diary, Reminiscences and Correspondence*, ed. by Thomas Sadler (1869).
ROSWITHA: *Plays*, trans. by H. J. Tillyard (1923).

SACKVILLE AND NORTON: *Gorboduc, or Ferrex and Porrex*, ed. by L. Toulmin-Smith (1883).
SAINTE-BEUVE, C. A.: *Portraits of the Seventeenth Century*, trans. by Katharine T. Wormeley (1904).

SAINTSBURY, GEORGE: *A Short History of French Literature* (1917); *Dryden* (1881).
SAND, MAURICE: *Masques et Buffons* (1860).
SAYLER, OLIVER M.: *The Russian Theatre* (1922).
SCHELLING, F. E.: *Elizabethan Playwrights* (1925).
SCHLEGEL, A. W.: *Lectures on Dramatic Art and Literature*, trans. by John Black (1871).
SCOLOKER, ANTHONY: *Daiphantus* (1604).
SCOTT, CLEMENT: *"The Bells" to "King Arthur"* (1895).
SCOTT, SIR WALTER: *Chivalry, Romance and the Drama* (1814); *Essay on Drama* (1819).
SENECA: *Tragedies*, trans. by E. J. Harris (1904).
SEYLER, ATHENE, AND HAGGARD, STEPHEN: *The Craft of Comedy* (1944).
SHAKESPEARE, WILLIAM: *Comedies, Histories and Tragedies*, ed. by John Heminge and Henry Condell ("First Folio," 1623); *Works*, ed. by Nicholas Rowe (1790); *Coriolanus*, adapted by Nahum Tate (1682); *Macbeth*, adapted by Sir William Davenant (1674); *The Merchant of Venice*, ed. by H. L. Withers (1896).
SHAW, G. BERNARD: *Dramatic Essays and Opinions* (1906); *Major Barbara* (Preface) (1907); *The Quintessence of Ibsenism* (1891).
SHIRLEY, JAMES: *The Contention of Ajax and Ulysses* (1659).
SHORT, ERNEST: *Theatrical Cavalcade* (1942).
SIDNEY, SIR PHILIP: *The Apologie for Poetry*, ed. by Edward Arber (1868).
SMITH, D. NICHOL: *Eighteenth Century Essays on Shakespeare*, ed. (1903).
SMITH, WINIFRED: *The Commedia dell' Arte* (1912).
SMYTH, HERBERT WEIR: *Aeschylus*, trans. (1922).
SOPHOCLES: *Tragedies*, trans. by E. H. Plumtre (1902); *Oedipus Rex*, trans. by Gilbert Murray (1910).
STANISLAVSKI, CONSTANTIN: *My Life in Art* (1925); *The Actor Prepares* (1936).
STEAD. W. T.: *The Passion Play at Oberammergau* (1910).
STEVENS, THOMAS: *The Theatres: From Athens to Broadway* (1932).
STOKER, BRAM.: *Personal Reminiscences of Henry Irving* (1906).
SULLIVAN, MARY: *Court Masques of James I* (1913).
SWINBURNE, ALGERNON CHARLES: *The Age of Shakespeare* (1908); *Contemporaries of Shakespeare* (1909); *A Study of Ben Jonson* (1889).
SYKES, H. DUGDALE: *Sidelights on Elizabethan Drama* (1924).
SYMONDS, J. ADDINGTON: *General Introduction to "Mermaid" Series* (1887); *Shakespeare's Predecessors in the English Drama* (1924).
SYMONS, ARTHUR: *Plays of Philip Massinger* (Preface) (1887).

TAGORE, SIR RABINDRANATH: *"Sacrifice" and Other Plays* (1917).

TASSO, TORQUATO: *Aminta*, trans. by John Reynolds (1628).
TERENCE: *Plays*, trans. by John Sarjeaunt (1912).
TERRY, DAME ELLEN: *Memoirs*, ed. by Edith Craig and Christopher
    St. John (1933).
TERTULLIAN: *De Spectaculis*, trans. by T. R. Glover (1931).
THEOPHRASTUS: *Characters*, trans. by Sir Richard Jebb, rev. by
    J. E. Sandys (1909).
THIRLWALL, BISHOP: *Essays* (1877).
TOULMIN-SMITH, L.: *York Plays* (1885).
TRENCH, R. C.: *The Life and Genius of Calderon* (1880).
TREWIN, J. C.: *The English Theatre* (1948).

ULRICI, HERMANN: *Shakespeare's Dramatic Art*, trans. by L. Dora
    Smitz (1876).
USTINOV, PETER: *Plays about People* (1950).

VAUGHAN, C. E.: *Types of Tragic Drama* (1908).
VERRALL, A. W.: *Euripides the Rationalist* (1895).
VOLTAIRE, F. M. AROUET DE: *Introduction to Semiramis* (1748).

WALKLEY, A. B.: *Drama and Life* (1907).
WARD, SIR ADOLPHUS: *A History of English Dramatic Literature* (1899).
WATSON, ERNEST BRADLEE: *Sheridan to Robertson* (1926).
WAXMAN, SAMUEL MONTEFIORE: *Antoine and the Théâtre Libre* (1926).
WHITMAN, WILLSON: *Bread and Circuses* (1938).
WIENER, LEO: *The Contemporary Drama of Russia* (1924).
WILKINSON, SIR JOHN: *A Popular Account of the Ancient Egyptians*
    (1890).
WILSON, A. E.: *Christmas Pantomime* (1934).
WILSON, J. DOVER: *The Essential Shakespeare* (1932).
WINTER, WILLIAM: *Henry Irving* (1885).
WRIGHT, T., AND HALLIWELL, J. O.: *Reliquiae Antiquae* (1841).
WYNDHAM, HENRY SAXE: *The Annals of Covent Garden Theatre*
    (1906).

INDEX